# GUTTUSO

Italian Presidency of the Council of the European Union

*1996*

The exhibition was organised by the Whitechapel Art Gallery, London
by the Civiche Gallerie d'Arte Moderna e Contemporanea di Ferrara
and by the Archivi Guttuso in Rome
Patronage of the Foreign Ministry of the Italian Republic

*editorial direction*
Domitilla Alessi

*editorial coordination*
Marco Carapezza
*english edition*
Catherine Lampert
Rebecca Hurst

*graphic project*
Marco Pennisi

*translations*
Denis Gailor
Maria Grazia Tornabene

*photocomposition*
Neuma, Palermo

*photos*
Bardazzi, Firenze
Enzo Brai - Publifoto, Palermo
Richard Bland, Washington
Giuseppe Cappellani, Palermo
Colorvaghi
Foto RCR, Parma
Padovan, Torino
Prudence Cuming
Associates Ltd., London
Giuseppe Schiavinotto, Roma
Saporetti, Milano
Studio Dabbrescia, Milano

*photolito*
Litoscanner, Palermo

*printing*
Priulla s.r.l., Palermo

©1996, Novecento Editrice
Via Siracusa, 16
90141 Palermo

First Published in Great Britain
in 1996 by Thames and Hudson
Ltd, London

British Library Cataloguing-in-
Publication Data
A catalogue record for this book
is available from the British Library

ISBN 0-500-97444-6

*official sponsor*
**BANCA DI ROMA**
GRUPPO CASSA DI RISPARMIO DI ROMA

Official Carrier

# GUTTUSO

Whitechapel Art Gallery, London, 17 may - 7 july        Civiche Gallerie, Ferrara, 20 july - 8 september

Novecento / Thames and Hudson

The purpose of an exhibition is to draw attention to a concept, a critical idea, and to offer a new perspective through the eloquence of pictures and documents. When the works displayed succeed in challenging deep-rooted stereotypes, forcing us to look with different eyes at periods and figures of a recent past, then the organizational effort can be considered as truly worthwhile.

It is significant that two galleries like the Whitechapel Art Gallery and the Civiche Gallerie d'Arte Moderna e Contemporanea di Ferrara, belonging to two culturally and geographically different places, and having very different traditions regarding Renato Guttuso, can today dedicate to him an exhibition, conceived jointly and organised in collaboration with the Archivi Guttuso in Rome.

This exhibition, selected by Sarah Whitfield, could ideally be entitled "Guttuso: painter". It aims to draw attention once again to the intensely pictorial quality of his work, and his unquestionably expressive energy, on which critical light is shed by the essays by Maurizio Calvesi and Sarah Whitfield, who reconstruct Guttuso's trajectory as a painter in twentieth-century art.

A figure who caused offence to some, Renato Guttuso was a complex artist and intellectual engaged on all fronts in the cultural debate of his day, and one who carried on an intense dialogue with the most authoritative voices in twentieth-century European culture. Bearing witness to the intensity and extent of the links between him and other intellectuals is the long list of prestigious names appearing in the fascinating reconsctruction that Massimo Onofri gives us of the relations between Guttuso and Italian writers. But, like few other painters, Guttuso provoked conflicting opinions, and was at the centre of polemic and debate, reflecting an epoch which is now over. No one else in Italy was subjected to as many diatribes in which there was an evident failure to separate the ideological component from the aesthetic one. But, as an authoritative critic Werner Haftmann has asserted, "realism in a doctrinaire sense had nothing to do with Guttuso", and his importance in the panorama of contemporary art "lies in the firmness with which he looked at the polarity of the real in order to transcend it in the exploration of the metaphysical and the allegorical". Particularly significant, in this connection, is Guttuso's relation with London. The lively exchange of the 'fifties, which was of major importance for two cultures which are so different, was cut short by ideological prejudices which led many artists and critics, as James Hyman's carefully written essay highlights, to condemn Guttuso for his ideas, and to condemn his paintings too.

Now that Guttuso has been dead for almost ten years and the passion which he aroused can be seen as spent, the time has come to mend the broken thread, in order to avoid a distorted vision outlasting not only Guttuso himself but also the end of certain ideological clashes.

If Guttuso is returning to London, as it were, in a climate which is decidedly different from that of the late 'fifties, he is also 'returning' to Ferrara, a city with which the artist had a continuous rapport over the years, culminating in the exhibition "Renato Guttuso. Immagini autobiografiche e altre opere", held in 1968 at the Palazzo dei Diamanti.

Thanks to the generosity of the lenders, many of whom knew Guttuso, an exhibition of both major and unfamiliar works has been realized.

The common intent of the Whitechapel Art Gallery, the Gallerie Civiche d'Arte Moderna e Contemporanea di Ferrara and the Archivi Guttuso, has been to offer a perspective on Guttuso's art allowing it to be judged in an objective manner, linked to the ability that the painter had to represent his own epoch, with the tools of his own art, to which he was tied by a more intense faith than that which connected him to any external ideology. Echoing this is a sentence of his which might constitute the manifesto of any Guttuso exhibition, but is particularly relevant to this one: "If the Eternal Father allowed me to choose a moment in history, and a craft, I would choose this time and the craft of a painter."

*Andrea Buzzoni*, Civiche Gallerie d'Arte Moderna e Contemporanea di Ferrara
*Fabio Carapezza Guttuso*, Archivi Guttuso, Roma
*Catherine Lampert*, Whitechapel Art Gallery, London

# Renato Guttuso's Journey

*Maurizio* **Calvesi**

Renato Guttuso was the most "popular" painter that Italian art produced in the twentieth century, and "popular" in two senses: in the sense that his success and notoriety with a vast public - that is his popularity - were exceptional, in a country which, by and large, has always been rather indifferent towards contemporary art, as it is in the myth of the great art of the past. He was the only major artist who, within a formal language, placed at the centre of his work existential and social themes which were rich in narrative references and largely accessible.

These characteristics have caused some Italian critics - supporters of the ciphered codes of the avant-garde - to look somewhat suspiciously on Guttuso, failing to notice not only his potent qualities, but also the profoundly "cultivated" nature of his idiom. They have as well overlooked the fundamental contribution he made to Italian art, including avant-garde art, by way of the expressionist modes of the thirties and later with his interest in Picasso, throughout the forties and the fifties.

At that time, indeed, Guttuso was the leader of a movement which, specifically bearing in mind the legacy of the Spanish artist, developed the potential of so-called "post-cubism", thus giving a precise impulse to the abstract research which for some years, after the Second World War, was oriented, in Italy as elsewhere, towards the breaking down of the composition into geometrical modules.

Guttuso, instead, remained faithful to the principles of figuration, leaving behind post-cubism and directing the expressionist idiom first towards social comment and then towards the narrative of daily life. His outspoken sympathy and feeling kept alive a line of research which today, in the return to figuration by so many young artists, has an undoubted topicality.

I met Renato Guttuso during the major Picasso exhibition at the Galleria Nazionale d'Arte Moderna in Rome in 1953 (with one hundred and seventy paintings and sculptures), which afterwards transferred to Milan. This was a major event for Italian art, which at that time was immersed in the fierce debate between realist and abstract artists. Each of the opposing groups saw in the works of the Spanish artist convincing arguments in favour of their own positions, while the press, still dominated by a conservative vision, thundered against the putative monstrosities of contemporary art, Picasso being considered its harmful promoter.

Together with my former teacher Lionello Venturi, Guttuso was a member of the executive committee and had been one of the people mainly responsible for putting on the exhibition, also made possible by his friendship with Picasso. I was at the start of my career and was part of the organisational staff. I remember meetings of the committee, and the tense atmosphere; Guttuso and Venturi quarrelled bitterly, although a few years before, at the time of the "Fronte nuovo delle arti", the critic had been a defender of the artist, whom he had presented at the 1948 Biennale.

By then polemics, marked by a high degree of passion, had divided them. Venturi became the supporter of the so-called "abstract-concrete" tendency - in which the abstract arrangement was enlivened by allusions, above all through colour, to the spectacle of nature. Guttuso did not appreciate this formula, which seemed indecisive and reductive to him, and instead aimed at an explicit continuation of that figurative experience with a strong sculptural inclination, but with an uneasy and creased character - so different from the drawing styles of the 'Novecento' painters - with which he had achieved renown in his youthful years. He had achieved his position precisely as a painter going against the tide confronting the puristic, backward-looking and sometimes rhetorical climate of those Italian explorations led by Carrà, Casorati, Campigli and Sironi, which went from the time of "Valori plastici" to the mural painting of the thirties.

His roots were - though in opposing diversity - in that climate of figurative research, and he refused to betray them, unlike Carrà or Casorati, but also the younger artists Morandi, Campigli, Marino Marini, or Giacomo Manzù (who was more or less the same age as Guttuso). Even the monumental experience of the mural, which greatly affected Italian painting in the thirties, though without involving Guttuso, contributed something to his artistic programme: something, once again, in terms of opposition. This related to a polemical confrontation, that occurred without rejecting large-scale composition but only its traditional stylistic rhetoric.

Indeed throughout Guttuso's vast production, starting from *Fuga dall'Etna* (Flight from Etna), which dates from the end of the thirties, until the late years - at regular intervals - he produced exceptionally large works. With these the painter sought a kind of continuity with the commitment, also in terms of composition, of the artists of the past. In this respect he cited Michelangelo, Caravaggio and Goya (who were in turn the models that inspired the muralists), and to whom he ideally linked Picasso's *Guernica*.

The exhibition includes a few examples of these grand paintings, which are also the best known ones; but rightly it gives some space, indeed above all, to "easel" paintings, in which there appear concentrated the requisites of Guttuso's incisive vision - which warps and at once respects reality, that is to say superimposes impetuous imagination on the motif - as well as of his explosive yet refined use of colour.

The artist's colour is by nature vehement and extrovert, however at times it retreats and expresses the intimate poetry of objects, indeed its own tormented intimacy. The - almost naturalistic - power of the sign and of volume remains an invariable trait of all his painting, often disruptive; but sometimes modified by contemplation, or, in the late period, by overwhelmingly bitter thoughts, when the force becomes the form, precisely, of this bitterness.

His success was enviable, and much envied by his fellow-artists; equally enviable was his physical appearance and his capacity to fascinate. Guttuso was a warm-blooded Southerner, with an open face and fine features, the brown complexion of that Sicilian stock which is mixed with ancient Arab ancestry, a fruity voice with robust timbres and a gaze which was frank, expressive, vibrant, passionate.

His culture was slightly old-fashioned and bourgeois, but liberal, inseparable from social commitment. It showed an all-round humanism related to literature. It came from his his mother who played the piano and his father who dabbled in poetry and painting, and was a militant socialist who boasted of ancestors who had supported Garibaldi. Behind Guttuso's spontaneous energy and confidence, he hid the hypochondria of a romantic intellectual, concealing unconfessed anguishes. A gentleman and generous by nature, ready to give and to give of himself, like someone who loves to be loved by everyone, Guttuso nevertheless harboured in his soul a certain solitude, to which he responded by continually waving the pencil or the brush, exhibiting an optimism meant to deny his inborn Sicilian pessimism, and a vitality which however "felt" death in a terrible way.

Picasso,
Guernica, 1937.
Museo Nacional de Arte
Reina Sofia, Madrid.

Renato Guttuso's first paintings date from the mid-twenties, and by the end of that decade he had already evolved a solid, indeed powerful style, stronger than that of Carrà, who was then the dominant figure, and certainly less schematic. In the colour-infused masses it reflected other possible influences, for example Funi, Menzio or Tozzi. The vehemence and energy of the young artist's composition compares only to the sculptures of Arturo Martini. It made him one of the less academic representatives of the new sculptural trend in Italian painting. *La donna del marinaio* (The sailor's woman), a painting done when he was twenty (1932), reflects this tendency, introducing a "romantic" component. The strong contrasts in the painting of the sky and sea suggest unease and deep feeling.

Guttuso has always been regarded as reacting against the stagnation of "Novecento" in a polemical fashion, and indeed he was soon to do just that. But the sculptural weight of his early works, which in a sense reflects twentieth-century culture, is already distinguished in the strongly expressive rôle of the colour, which remained an inalienable and fundamental trait in the subsequent development of his work.

A few years later, the *Autoritratto con sciarpa e ombrello* (Self-portrait with scarf and umbrella, 1936) shows the development achieved in common with the expressionist mood of the "Roman school" but also through the study of old masters like El Greco. (This attention to painting of the past, which extended to Van Gogh and Cézanne - of whom he did likenesses - is characteristic of Guttuso. He liked to enter into a dialogue with the history of art, which he vividly felt to have a living presence).

In the *Self-portrait*, the sense of sculptural construction is still marked, and wholly resolved into the fullness of the colour. However, the planes move and the volumes are as if tormented by an interior power, bearing the impression of an agitated vitality which is simultaneously manifest in the intensity of the tones. Guttuso's natural restlessness comes to terms with ideological uneasiness; it rebels against the oppression of fascism, in a stormy period which opens with the Spanish Civil War, and ends with the Second World War.

*Fucilazione in campagna* (Execution in the country, 1938) confronts a theme which is now decidedly political. As a bitter comment, red, the dominant colour of the painter's inflamed imagination, is translated into the spectacle of blood and takes on sombre reverberations. The figures are sketched and the tight composition grows dense in just a few areas, loosely heightening the drama by its own disconnected force.

The imminent catastrophe is announced by the representation of calamitous events, as in *Flight from Etna*, or by religious images used as a transparent metaphor of the massacre taking place, as in the *Crucifixion*. The two more or less contemporaneous paintings (1938-40 and 1940-1) hark back to two different ideas of a pictorial stage: agitated action, represented by extreme agitation, and the suspension of the tragic, in a petrified action. In *Flight from Etna* the wedge-shaped composition contains two converging diagonals, with the fallen figure or the chair overturned in the middle, which seems to be borrowed from Caravaggio's *Martyrdom of St. Matthew*. In the *Crucifixion* the downward movement of the bodies creates a more rigid structure, dramatised by the tension of the forms and by the red accents (the chromatically transfigured body of the thief) which contrast with the white or ashy tones.

These two paintings are among the most formidable testimonies that art has given us to the anguish and inhumanity of the Second World War. And it is natural that in endeavouring to bear witness, Guttuso should feel drawn to a work like *Guernica*, although in these paintings the formal language of Picasso is not yet used. His influence, however, was apparent immediately afterwards, or almost in the same months, in other works like *Le ragazze di Palermo* (The girls of Palermo, a title intentionally echoing *Les demoiselles d'Avignon*) or the splendid *Ritratto di Mimise con il cappello rosso* (Portrait of Mimise with red hat).

Guttuso's interest in Picasso preceded *Guernica*, as is demonstrated by the enthusiastic articles he devoted to the father of cubism in 1933, in the Sicilian newspaper *L'Ora*, which have only recently been found and published once again. What Guttuso wrote is no doubt surprising, not only for the critical intuition, unique in Italy at that time; but also in relation to the kind of painting which occupied him.

At first sight, it is difficult to detect any influence of Picasso, unless we detect a trace of the "neoclassical" Picasso in the monumental quality of an image like *The sailor's woman*, whose pose reminds one of the 1920 *Femme assise* (Musée Picasso, Paris), or in details like the big hands of the 1936 *Self-Portrait*. This parallel remains problematic, but cannot altogether be ruled out.

With respect to the *Crucifixion*, it is also possible that in painting it Guttuso had in mind the work on the same subject done ten years earlier by the Spanish artist: and yet the differences could not be more marked, apart from

Guttuso,
The girls of Palermo, 1940.
Galleria Nazionale d'Arte Moderna,
Rome.

the theme, the expressionist contrast of the colours, and the details (though conventional in terms of iconography) of the steps, present in some preparatory drawings, and the dice ostentatiously on view in the foreground.

In terms of composition, in a beautiful study for the *Crucifixion* in India ink and watercolour, the figure on the left - a rearing horse with rider - might correspond to the large figure with the monumental head which in Picasso's painting is also to the left of the crucified man. But Guttuso's is an image which replaces Picasso's deformation with the dramatic rendering of representation, introducing the figurative theme which later was to be the one especially favoured by Marino Marini: that of the rearing horse with rider.

In the final version of the *Crucifixion* the animal stands out in the foreground, with its nostrils turned backwards. This is an addition which might derive from the other painting by Picasso which Guttuso knew from a postcard he had received in 1939 from his friend the critic Cesare Brandi, who was travelling in the United States – and that painting was *Guernica*.

Although Guttuso had known and admired Picasso's painting for many years, he never imitated his style. He chose to seize the dramatic quality of his works, for the moment when that dramatic quality had become the mirror of living history, the face of history itself, its trait, its bloody idiom. And as a bloody idiom, not as a mere stylistic trait or cerebral arabesque, Guttuso then took on Picasso's "influence", as if taking stock of the profound convergence of his message with the tragedy taking place in the world. Yet this influence did not in the least alter the structure of Guttuso's painting, nurtured on colour precisely as if it were blood and flesh, and made up of masses subjected to an expressionistic upheaval but never reduced to the linear frame, to the disembodied and violently abstract grammar of Picasso's model.

The fact that Guttuso looks forward to Marino Marini, as mentioned, is already a clear sign of the influence that Guttuso, through his interest in Picasso, was to have on much Italian art in the forties, a decade in which the Sicilian artist was the greatest and most advanced protagonist of the formal language explored in our country.

In the series of interiors, still lifes and portraits done in 1941-4, objects and characters are invested with the same liveliness. Inside the plastic granite block, the three-dimensionality of which Guttuso does not renounce - since it is "realistically" necessary, and necessary as a vast field of impact, and also as the breathing space of the colour - violent gaps translate into big irregular prisms the broken rhythms of the incipient "post-cubist" idiom - an idiom which, according to its own intrinsic logic, is conceived of as two-dimensional.

When this syntax begins to become more recognisable, as in *Il merlo* (The blackbird) or in the new *Portrait of Mimise* or in the decidedly Picassian *Cucitrici* (Seamstresses, 1947), the subtlety tends to diminish, while the dramatic impetuosity of the sign is attenuated in the contemplation of a more cerebral and geometrical architecture of forms, and the colour tends to become precious, laid out on flatly painted surfaces which wind in ribbon-fashion or penetrate one another in inlaid fashion.

And yet the profundity, though reduced, is never cancelled out, there is not that total distension of the composition transferred to the surface which we can find, already in the same year, in a painter like Giulio Turcato or in a sculptor such as Consagra, to mention two artists who were close to Guttuso, who helped and supported them, since at that time they were less well known. (Guttuso did particularly successful portraits of each of them.) They also shared the same political viewpoint, and the closeness of Turcato to Guttuso at that time can be discerned in the themes of his painting, like *The blackbird* or *La presa delle terre* (The taking of land).

Thus it was not political ideology that caused the subsequent divergence between realism and abstract art. This divergence was already implicit, precisely, in the different approach to the new decompositional syntax and in Guttuso's avoidance of the two-dimensional flattening found in the post-cubist model which was the mental premise of the abstract idiom.

In Guttuso the idea of "commitment" did nothing but add an ideological dimension to what was a deeply rooted expressive and cultural need, deriving from his very formation.

Hence Guttuso at that time (1947) was a leading figure in an important Italian movement, expressed in the "Fronte nuovo delle arti", with Franchina (another friend of his from Sicily, like Consagra), Turcato himself, Birolli, Leoncillo, Morlotti, Pizzinato, Vedova, Santomaso, Viani, Fazzini and Corpora.

After the 1947 exhibition at the Galleria della Spiga in Milan, the group presented their works the following year at the Venice Biennale, but they disbanded soon afterwards.

Guttuso,
Portrait of Giulio Turcato and the cat
Molotov, 1946.
Private collection.

Certainly the least happy period in Guttuso's long career - though not one devoid of fascinating moments - is the period (lasting a decade) of programmatic "realism", which began in 1949 with progressive retreat from post-cubist experimentation and the search for a more naturalistic form, though sculptural in an elementary way, congenial to a vein of folk narration. Through this vein the painter recovered the memory of the Sicilian carts, with the lively colours and simple narrative imagery. His first teacher had been a painter of carts.

Large works with epic intentions, like *La battaglia di Ponte dell'Ammiraglio* (The Ponte dell'Ammiraglio battle, 1951-2), present the most popular Italian hero, Garibaldi, as a model of combativeness who aimed at the social liberation of peasants and workmen, in years of bitter political struggles. In works of this kind, the clear and articulated rigidity of the figures succeeds in bringing together the memory of the Sicilian cart (with its naive puppet-like figures) with the compositional shrewdness of robust and plastic means, giving rise to a singular form of painterly invention, as original as it is pleasantly anachronistic. This is a phase which is wholly indicative of Guttuso's personality and it is still waiting to be understood and re-evaluated.

The clearly outlined circular form of *Boogie Woogie* (1953) has the same dancing regularity within a more airy impetus, and with a rhythmic form acutely echoed in the depiction, in the background, of the abstract painting by Mondrian with the same title. It is meant as a portrait of "modernity" and has all the optimistic flavour of the fifties.

Among the finest works of the decade are the Sicilian landscapes, with the spectacle of a dense sea, thick orange

Guttuso,
Blackbird, 1947.
Galleria Nazionale d'Arte Moderna,
Rome.

18

groves and twisted prickly-pear plants, where the palette and the painter's touch seem to find a spontaneous correspondence in the shapes and colours of the natural scene, thus almost documenting the fact that they originate from the observation of nature which is imaginatively interpreted.

With the start of the sixties political commitment had come to an end, the artist's vision was more serene and he seemed to concentrate wholly on his reflections on the reasons for painting. A picture which may appear emblematic is *Tetti su Via Leonina* (Roofs over Via Leonina), done in 1962, where the construction of skilfully arranged spaces and the harmony of colours seem to take us back to the structural and post-cubist explorations of the forties, which however are modified by an air of contemplation. No less significant is the series of still lifes inspired by Giorgio Morandi, which continue to 1965.

Between the spring and summer of 1965, Guttuso painted the "autobiographical cycle", including thirty-six paintings as well as a large number of drawings and watercolours. These are moments of his life welling up as memories and are a significant withdrawal from his fierce contact with everyday life. Recollection at times appears as limpid as an autumn day, and at others fades away into a dream.

*Gioacchino Guttuso agrimensore* (Gioacchino Guttuso land-surveyor) is the title of the portrait of his father. It is a masterpiece of penetration, in the way it suggests the dignified, rigorous personality of this man intent on his own precise work, while on a tall tripod, which is like an indicator of his upright station, he adjusts the measuring device.

Guttuso,
Boogie-Woogie, 1953.
Private collection.

The dome of the umbrella protects him against the scorching sun, whose reverberations are caught in the grass in the field. The sky is rendered with a deep, compact blue, which causes the pallor of the face to stand out. The distribution of the colours is wholly invented, though without attenuating the truth, above all psychological, of the image, which indeed proves to be intensified by it.

*Il pittore di carretti* (The cart painter) evokes Guttuso's first teacher. The figure is faceless, as if conjured up from memory, with only the hand gripping the brush. The effect is extraordinarily intense.

From this moment on, the critical categories of "realism" and "expressionism", into which people have attempted to make Guttuso's painting fit, prove more approximate and inadequate than ever.

Henceforth he can be seen as a great isolated figure, both nationally and internationally, intent on forging a kind of painting that we could continue to call "narrative" but in many cases is "confessional", while in others it is characterised by evocation. In any event, there is always a dialogue: with himself, as in the 1978 "allegories", or *Passeggiata in giardino a Velate* (A walk in the garden in Velate, 1983); with his own private world, as in *La visita della sera* (The evening visit, 1980); with the spectacle of life, as in the splendid *Vucciria*, 1974; with the great figures from the past, as in *Il convivio* (The banquet, 1973), or *Van Gogh porta il suo orecchio al bordello di Arles* (Van Gogh delivering his ear to the brothel in Arles, 1978); with history, in the way he interweaves past and present, as in *Il Caffè Greco* (1976).

Guttuso,
Gioacchino Guttuso,
land-surveyor, 1966.
Galleria Renato Guttuso,
Bagheria, PA.

20

Picture by picture he built up a grand fresco from which the autobiographical or at least "private" component cannot be eliminated, and in which reflection takes the place of expressionism.

The handling, though still sculpturally tense, takes into account the slower, more pondered thought processes, no longer has a force of impact, a violence of direct "entry" into things, but derives from a more considered construction born of meditation, from a sort of montage which observes the slower and graver process of contemplation; and, lastly, from a process of "re-composition" which takes the place of the newly-absorbed broken syntax.

These slower and more grandiose times, this graver movement, correspond, in psychological terms, to the entrenched sadness which gripped the artist and which led to alternating states between the calm of melancholy and the drama of anguish. The subject is now Guttuso's "own" drama and is no longer that of the world, and no longer drama in the etymological sense of action.

A painting like *The evening visit*, with its exceptional poetic intensity and almost metaphysical pace, may appear to stand outside the *oeuvre* only to those who misunderstand the change in his relations with the world which occurs in the late work: a relationship no longer consisting of "intervening" but of "passiveness" - in taking on the role of a spectator, in receiving, and hence also in contemplating in a more relaxed way. *The evening visit* is a portrait of the artist's "evening", of his solitude which is more disturbed than comforted by contacts which can be predacious, by tiring events. And everything, I repeat, becomes autobiography (sometimes overt autobiography), even a painting like

Guttuso,
The cart painter, 1966.
Private collection.

the one portraying Van Gogh in the brothel, with his pitiful mutilation; and here too we can see how the architecture of the narration attenuates or eliminates the violence of the brushstroke.

Guttuso in his last twenty years, and even more in his last ten years, is in a sense a novelist, fundamentally close (in the same city) to his friend and admirer Alberto Moravia. It is not by chance that the latter wrote about him, just as Guttuso portrayed him several times, the last time in 1982. The two appear to have much in common, both in terms of their life stories and in their need for an objectivity with psychological overtones, as in the theme of women and sex. Moravia, however, differed in that his wisdom, which was an expression of a certain coldness, defended him like a suit of armour, while Guttuso was always exposed, both in the "interventions" of his more intense years and in the "passiveness" of his long twilight. And he was animated by a warmer pathos, warm like the colours of his land, like the fire of Etna, like the turquoise of the Tyrrhenian Sea, like the green of the lizards and the twisted vegetation, like the yellow of the oranges and sulphur, which were always the colours of his palette.

If we wish to correctly "place" Renato Guttuso's painting, we must, I would like to stress once more, evaluate its deep roots: firstly, the "objective" sculptural quality of the Italian school of the twenties, then the impact with expressionism and Picasso as the champion of violent and jarring modernity (but not to the extent of interfering with the original powerful sculptural roots), and not reducible to the abstraction of art for art's sake, but instead to be enjoyed as the persistent search for a form of figurative art; lastly the expansiveness of the colour, an almost

Guttuso,
The Caffé Greco, 1976.
Ludwig Collection, Köln.

"Mediterranean", indeed Sicilian, vision, and that "literary" component, implicit in his humanistic education, which always prevented him from separating painting from narrative. This led to his being substantially isolated, leaving him increasingly alone amidst the manifold experiments of the avant-garde, as it abandoned first the figure and then painting itself. The only true parallel with his art lies in the personalities of writers such as Moravia who, in an era like the post-war period, insisted on art as an autonomous experiment with idiom.

Guttuso,
The evening visit, 1980.
Galleria Nazionale
d'Arte Moderna, Rome.

*following page:*
Guttuso,
Still life with red cloth, 1942.
Private collection.

# Seeing Red

*Sarah* **Whitfield**

*Guttuso fixes his gaze on the object obsessively,*
*like the bull on the red rag.*

Alberto Moravia

Guttuso's position late in life as an elected representative of the people - he was made a Senator of the Republic in 1976 - was a public tribute to an artist who for the past forty years had steadfastly practised his belief that art should be of its own time, accessible to all, and above all, `useful'.[1]

Guttuso became politically active during the German occupation of Italy as a member of a military organisation of Partisans operating in Central Italy. Before that, however, his studio had become the meeting place for a small band of intellectuals critical of Italy's Fascist regime. In 1940 he joined the clandestine Italian Communist Party and remained a regular and charismatic speaker at political debates and public meetings. From an early age he was also a prolific writer of newspaper articles and important essays on art and culture.

His art was championed by two of the finest Italian novelists of this century, Alberto Moravia and Leonardo Sciascia, and his praises sung by virtually all the famous names among Italian art critics and historians (like Garibaldi, Guttuso was a prophet who was honoured in his own country). Bernard Berenson hailed him as `the last painter in the great tradition of Italian art'. Outside Italy his reputation flourished in both Eastern and Western Europe. He was awarded the Lenin Prize for Peace and Friendship between Nations on the occasion of a major retrospective in Moscow in 1972. In England he was supported first by Douglas Cooper (an enormously influential critic who had drawn attention to Guttuso's painting as early as 1948),[2] and then by the leading Marxist critic of modern art, John Berger, who wrote the introduction of his show at the Leicester Galleries in 1955 (and a monograph which was published in

Dresden in 1957), and by the philosopher Richard Wollheim at the time of Guttuso's third London one-man show in 1960.[3] When he had his first exhibition in America in 1958, Cooper and James Thrall Soby, another internationally powerful critical voice, both contributed to the catalogue.

Nevertheless, if a visitor to the Tate Gallery today were asked what they thought of Guttuso's painting the question would probably draw a blank. It could hardly be otherwise. There has not been an exhibition of his work in this country since 1979,[4] and there is very little published about him in English; few museums outside Italy regularly show the paintings by him in their collections. The reason for this lack of interest, one suspects, is that nowadays the work is seen as marginal, even a little old-fashioned: it fits uneasily into surveys of twentieth-century painting. Guttuso was a painter committed to the Communist cause who worked within a strong Italian tradition of public art and of public awareness of art. In Britain, however, which does not have a strong tradition of public art, there is a very limited audience for large politically engaged paintings and still less for paintings that deal with social issues such as the occupation by Sicilian labourers of uncultivated land, the urban terrorism of the Mafia, the war in Vietnam. Moreover, Guttuso's works do not pander to the European taste for *belle peinture* (Soby called him 'an ungraceful artist' and Berger refers to his 'impatient crudeness').[5] For this reason alone his paintings can look brash and out of place when hung with works by other, more refined painters.

But if writers and museum curators outside Italy have found Guttuso's art unaccommodating, they have nonetheless

Guttuso,
The young Picasso
in Barcelona, 1957.
Private collection.

recognised the vital importance of the chief question it poses: how to make figurative art in a post-cubist world? As Richard Wollheim put it: 'Guttuso has realised - as someone who has truly absorbed a theory like Marxism should have - that representation is, in part at least, a historical problem'.[6]

Alberto Moravia asserted that the only way in which a painter working in the modern world could be a figurative artist (he was writing in 1962) was to be an expressionist.[7] What he meant by that becomes clear when he describes Guttuso's affinity with 'another Mediterranean expressionist', Picasso. He pointed out that theirs was an expressionism founded on 'fatality of blood, of pride, of the taste for power and cruelty'. It was an affinity that went beyond the bounds of modern painting or a common ideology, that came out of 'roots in a common atavistic past'.[8] When Guttuso paid tribute to Picasso in his work by incorporating figures from his paintings (in *The shipwrecked*, *Flight from Etna* and *Crucifixion*, for instance), or his likeness, the act of doing so is a gesture of fraternal solidarity. The language Moravia uses to define the expressionism common to Guttuso and Picasso (and it is fair to assume that Guttuso would not have quibbled with his choice of words) is the language of violence: blood, pride, power, cruelty. These words are particularly appropriate in the case of Guttuso, although, as Moravia also pointed out: 'There is something warm, generous and down-to-earth in Guttuso's violence'.[9] With the exception of early works in the classical spirit of the Italian Novecento movement of the 1920s, such as *Palinurus* and *The shipwrecked*, the subjects, the choice of objects, the execution, all bear witness to Guttuso's taste for violent expression. Picasso's art presents

Guttuso,
Hammer and red hat, 1940–41.
Private collection.

an altogether different case. While he believed that art should be `an instrument of attack and defence against the enemy', there is (as Guttuso himself observed) a pronounced dialectic in his work between violence and tenderness, a dialectic which is conspicuously absent from Guttuso's own painting.

One has only to look at the objects he depicts to see to what extent Guttuso's painting is devoid of any mark, any touch that could be construed as a caress. He sets out to instill a sense of danger and discomfort by revealing the natural world to be as hazardous and harmful as the man-made. The ripe and downy fruits of European still-life painting are replaced by the spiky forms of cacti, chestnuts, artichokes, lobster and sea urchins, by the hard bulbous heads and coarse leaves of cauliflowers, by the unappetising dryness of red-hot peppers. Tangled branches of lemon and olive trees obstruct the surface of the canvas as effectively as a barrier of barbed wire. Everyday objects are equally threatening: hammers and sharp pincers, scissors and forks, piles of wrecked metal, open tin cans, objects that repel the human instinct to reach out and touch.

In 1942, a year or so after Guttuso has painted the large *Crucifixion* and when he was engaged in some of the first large still-lifes, he wrote, `A crucifixion that resembles a still-life is a still-life that resembles a crucifixion. This is true of all real painting form the Byzantines to Caravaggio and to Picasso'[10] This declaration goes to the heart of the matter, for it could be argued that it was through the subject of the still-life that Guttuso found his most powerful means of expression. The analogy he makes between a still-life and a crucifixion is manifest in paintings such as

Guttuso,
Interior with cage 1940-41.
Private collection.

*Hammer and red hat* or *Corner of the studio* where symbols of the Passion - a hammer in one, a pair of pliers in the other - are given a conspicuous place amongst the studio clutter. In *Corner of the studio*, the view towards a hill darkening under a blood-red sky is another allusion to Christ's death. In *Interior with cage* painted at the same time as the *Crucifixion*, a pair of pliers is placed next to two heavy duty nails. In *La Vucciria*, one of the grandest of the paintings on a still-life theme and surely Guttuso's masterpiece of the late years, he employs a familiar metaphor for the crucified body of Christ in the large side of beef. This image of sacrifice (taken from Annibale Carracci's *The Butcher's Shop*) is made more terrible by the figure of the butcher calmly slicing through the flesh.

For the most part, though, the suffering conveyed through the still-lifes derives from the fact that, as Richard Wollheim observed, 'nature for Guttuso is essentially the human environment', a negative force 'frustrating human action'.[11] The jumble of objects in the later still-lifes, such as *Corner of the studio*, create a sense of frustration in that profusion and disorder, qualities which in a Dutch or Spanish still-life convey a sense of richness, opulence, permanence, here convey exactly the opposite. The studio paraphernalia are scruffy, worn, on the verge of being discarded, alarmingly unstable. (In his text 'L'insegnamento di Picasso' Guttuso points out that Picasso's art is revolutionary precisely because it seeks to break down the 'stable world').[12] The randomness of the composition of *Corner of the studio* generates unease, as it does in several of Cézanne's still-lifes (another prime source for Guttuso) where as many as eighteen or twenty apples lie scattered across the composition like balls on a snooker table. Here,

Anon.,
The Triumph of death, XV cent.
Galleria regionale della Sicilia,
Palermo.

29

the large scale, 180 x 229 cm., the lack of a single focal point, the sense of imminent collapse, create a dark mood of apprehension. Alienation from order and harmony is made even more evident in a later painting, *The breaker's yard*, 1979, one of Guttuso's bleakest comments on human waste. The negation and frustration Wollheim writes about are implicit in the choice of a place with no sense of place, with no vestiges of human life other than the metal shells of discarded vehicles. It is a desolate vision, a glimpse of man-made hell.

Nonetheless, it is a vision which is presented with grandeur, drama and passion. Each object Guttuso paints seems to increase in dignity under his hard intense scrutiny. In the still-lifes of the 1940s Guttuso concentrates on the trappings of Italian agricultural life: a straw hat, a wine flask, a bird cage, a wooden chair, roughly-made and worthless items which stand their ground with a sort of obstinacy. Indeed, it is the strength of that link with a specific society, and with its underlying violence, that gives these paintings without figures a vividly human presence. Just as in Van Gogh's painting of an empty chair the absence of a figure is part of the image, so in *Still-life with red cloth*, 1942, the gaping emptiness of the chair at the centre of the composition suggests an absence, a departure. This void is made more telling by the significance of the red cloth, a clandestine reference to the Red Flag.

The visible wear and tear suffered by objects in everyday use invests them with human attributes: the twisted pieces of straw unravelling from the seat of the chair in *Still-life with red cloth*, for instance, bring to mind the writhing fingers of Christ in Grünewald's Isenheim altarpiece. In general, though, tools, wine bottles, books, hats and cigarette

Guttuso,
The funeral of Togliatti 1972.
Galleria d'Arte Moderna, Bologna.

packets look as though they have just been thrown aside or hastily abandoned. Very few of the still-lifes are composed in the traditional manner of arranging objects on a flat surface. Guttuso constructs a still-life as though he were constructing a barricade. The brutal piling up of objects conveys the sense of a community trapped and impoverished, but there is also a sense of shared human activity, a universal solidarity conveyed through the crowding together of humble everyday necessities. The way in which objects are often placed on the ground with nothing between them and the earth reinforces the link between the painter and his native Sicilian land. The rawness of the subject matter, which evokes the harshness and smell of manual labour, is conveyed through the thick, unmodulated, broadly applied, workmanlike paint.

Guttuso, like Picasso, consciously evoked the continuity of art by paying homage to celebrated masterpieces. Whereas Picasso can be said to have tried to put himself in the place of Velasquez, Poussin, Manet, in order to take their paintings forward to new and unforeseen conclusions, Guttuso wanted to ensure the survival of representation and the tradition of making art a political act. He once said, 'I have always considered that the painter's honour lay in painting large pictures'.[13] In other words, the painter's `honour' required him to take up the challenge of history painting.

Guttuso identified the first of his modern history paintings as *Flight from Etna*, painted in 1938-39, when he was around 26 years old. But he had already painted a work which, although less heroic in scale, is in much the same

Guttuso,
Friends in the studio, 1940.
Private collection.
Left to right:
the collector Alberto della Ragione,
the painter Mario Mafai,
the critic Antonello Trombadori
and the painter Giulio Turcato.

spirit. *Execution in the country* is dedicated to the poet Federico Garcia Lorca, shot by the Nationalists during the Spanish Civil War. The scene of the cold-blooded killing is an echo of Goya's *The Third of May*, but the mood is elegiac rather than electrifying. The quiet acquiescence of the victims and the sombre muddy colours intensify the sense of futile violence.

*Flight from Etna after an eruption* also comes out of Goya, the surging mass of figures recalling the doomed crowds in the Black Paintings, and through this link with Spain, Guttuso makes another link with the recent horror of the Spanish Civil War. This painting is also in the tradition of the imposing crowd paintings realised by the Italian Futurists and before them, the Divisionists, notably Giuseppe Pelliza da Volpedo, whose epic painting, *The Fourth estate*, showed 'a crowd of people, workers of the soil...strong, robust, united.'[14] But the work of art that was the initial inspiration for this picture of mass terror was much more recent. It was, as Guttuso himself said, *Guernica*. The metaphor he found for the destruction unleashed by the Germans in April 1937 on the Basque town is the eruption of Sicily's volcanic Mount Etna, dimly seen behind the crowd of scrambling stumbling figures. The most specific allusion to the Picasso mural is the straining neck of the terrified horse which links one part of the group with the other. Guttuso was convinced that Picasso's model for the horse in *Guernica* was the skeletal animal ridden by Death in the anonymous Catalan mural *The triumph of Death*, originally in the Palazzo Sclafani, Palermo.[15]

In the more ambitious *Crucifixion* which followed a year or so later, Guttuso, who had recently joined the Partito Comunista d'Italia (PCdI), responded to the conditions of war and the increasingly powerful grip of Italy's Fascist government with a more conventional allegory of suffering. If this large canvas appears tame in comparison with figurative art being produced elsewhere in Europe around 1940 - by Max Beckmann in particular - it should be seen in the context of the task that Guttuso had set himself. `I want to speak clearly and to seem obvious without being obvious, and thus to say things that are totally new. I want to know how to make the most use of the discoveries of avant-garde art without copying the methods of others.'[16] Specific references to the `avant-garde' include a reworking of one of the most extreme gestures of grief in *Guernica* (hands beating the air), and a salute to the blue horses of Franz Marc. The high pitched palette is also a deliberate allusion to the strident reds and blues of the German Expressionists. The dominant colour, red, like the clenched fists of the crucified, is a coded reference to the defiance of the Communists under Fascism, while the apparent contradiction in broadcasting a Communist message through a Christian image is explained by the readiness of the Catholics and Communists in Italy to unite together against Fascism.[17]

The huge furore that greeted the *Crucifixion* when it was first shown in 1942 at the fourth Premio Bergamo, an official competition organised by Giuseppe Bottai, the Minister of National Education, was as much religious as political. Guttuso's offence was twofold: not only was the face of Christ obscured behind the cross bearing one of the thieves, but the Magdalene, reaching up to wipe away the blood from Christ's wound, was depicted as naked. In the eyes of the Church, and of many Italians, Guttuso had painted a work that was flagrantly blasphemous. And one has only to think of the fuss that greeted Martin Scorsese's film *The last temptation of Christ* in 1988 to comprehend the inflammatory nature of an image of a naked Magdalene in Italy in the early 1940s. The painting was excluded from official exhibitions in Italy up to the 1972 Venice Biennale.

One of the strongest tensions in Guttuso's work is his desire to deploy his considerable mastery of composition on a heroic scale, as he does here, and his desire to give full rein to his powers of invention and painterliness, as he does in the still-lifes mentioned above (*Corner of the studio* in particular), or in smaller canvases around the theme of war such as *Massacre*, *Battle and Wounded horses*, *Triumph of Death*. These modest paintings convey a dramatic immediacy that is somehow absent in the grand pictorial set pieces of the later years. While it is difficult not to applaud Guttuso's belief that an artist is a witness to the events of his own time and must assume the weight of that responsibility, canvases on the scale of *Documentary on Vietnam* (1965), *Newspaper-mural: May '68* (1968), *The funeral of Togliatti* (1972), although daring in conception and immensely skillful in execution, are tinged with the chilly clarity of propaganda. They do not move us in the way that the small battle scenes of the early 1940s do, compositions in which scenes of carnage are picked out like details from a much larger painting (Uccello's *The Rout of San Romano* comes to mind). Guttuso (like Picasso) evokes the barbarism of war through the traditional iconography of rearing horses, fallen bodies, splayed limbs, archetypal images spiced with details almost medieval in their horror.

Guttuso,
Roofs in Algiers, 1957.
Private collection.

Finding a contemporary idiom for traditional iconography was one of Guttuso's main tasks. Take *The discussion*. The subject is the group, a recurring theme which goes back to an early work such as *Friends in the studio* celebrating the close companionship and common purpose that had been an integral part of Guttuso's early life, first in Sicily and then in Milan with the *Corrente* group. It was a theme that Guttuso sometimes carried into the realm of myth or fantasy as in *The young Picasso in Barcelona*, an oil of 1957 showing the Spanish painter seated at a café table in the company of his friends; sometimes mixing fact with fiction, as in *Caffè Greco* and the ambitious late cycle of paintings, *Autobiography*. In *The discussion* the group is engaged in political debate. Pieces of German, French and Italian newspapers, roughly torn into shape before being glued to the surface, draw attention to words and names calculated to stir and inflame. Art is drawn into this discussion: the cover of a recent exhibition catalogue featuring a Léger painting is pasted to the surface some distance away from the truncated name of Giacometti. The powerful gestures of the protagonists, the crumpled newspaper, the real cigarette packet neatly positioned near the painted ashtray heaped with stale cigarette butts, set the scene in the style of an Italian film of the 1950s. But the sense of tempers suddenly flaring is expressed, above all, by the diagonal of the table driving through the centre of the group splitting the two sides wide apart. It is a powerful destabilizing device of the sort employed by masters of the dramatic moment like Tintoretto, Caravaggio or Guercino. And even though the figures are for the most part static, the dynamism of the group, the sense of jarring mental collision, the restlessness of the roughly collaged surface, bear out John Berger's observation that Guttuso was 'essentially a painter of movement.' The old-masterish quality of the composition is surely not fortuitous and it is tempting to see this painting as a reworking of a traditional subject in which figures are seated around a table. Guttuso may even have had in mind Caravaggio's *Supper at Emmaus*, in which the moment when Christ is recognised is depicted with a suddenness that splits the composition apart.

Another, earlier, example of Guttuso reworking traditional iconography is found in the modest-sized *Crucifixion in a room*. Here, the confined space of a small interior replaces the outdoor scene of Golgotha, evoking the airless prison cell and newer, equally terrible forms of dealing with religious and political dissidents.

Although Guttuso pursued a career outside contemporary taste and fashion, his paintings nonetheless reflect a curiosity about the art of his own time. This is most evident in the mid-1950s with works such as *Roofs in Algiers* or *Orange grove* which stop just short of the sort of quasi-abstraction that a painter like Nicolas de Staël, for instance, was practising a few years earlier, around 1951-52. Patterns made of the roof tiles and the leafy tops of fruit trees fill the canvas in dense stylized repetitions. The slabs of paint in *Roofs at Velate*, squares of yellow, orange and red roofs are crushed together beneath the sharp tangle of branches to create an impenetrable surface. Released from the demands of a more conventional figurative art, Guttuso pushes his subject as close as he can to the abstract painting of his own day short of compromising its legibility.

His appreciation of De Staël[18] has surely to do with that painter's use of his material. Guttuso's own technique is extremely robust (the collaged surface of *The discussion*, for instance, has the texture of a peeling wall) and robustness was a quality he admired in others. As Richard Wollheim has said, Guttuso 'grasped one of the most important and revolutionary lessons of cubist painting: namely, that the realism of a picture can be enhanced by emphasizing the reality of the painting.'[19] The same could be said about De Staël, whose involvement with the physical properties of paint, its soft consistency and its malleability evidently struck a chord with Guttuso. Maurizio Calvesi, who, while acknowledging Guttuso's horror of psychoanalytical readings of his work, finds significant a childhood memory related by the painter himself. In the studio of the Sicilian painter Domenico Quattrociocchi, where Guttuso was allowed to play undisturbed, he liked to touch and sniff and dirty himself with the scrapings of paint Quattrociocchi saved by moulding them together into round 'crostone'. Calvesi also saw the physical pleasure Guttuso took in handling paint as an (unconscious) act of defiance against his father, an amateur watercolourist, who objected to his son using oils because they were too messy.[20] Be that as it may, it is certainly the case that if Guttuso's paint is aggressive, even unpleasant at times, it is invariably handled with relish, not as a conventional tool of seduction, but as a way of keeping in touch with the messiness of daily life.

The messiness of daily life is also reflected in the large late drawings and paintings of nudes of 1970s. As early as 1962, Moravia had recognized Guttuso's ability to capture the squalor and loneliness of what he called "proletarian promiscuity".[21] The hardness and absence of feeling that Guttuso manages to convey through the late nudes are an

De Staël,
Fugue, 1951.
Phillips Collection, Washington.

eloquent equivalent to the atrophied emotions of the cheap picture book, the 'fumetti' found in every kiosk on every main street in Italy. As Guttuso grew older, wealthier, more celebrated, finding a way of making an art that continued to have a social and political validity seems to have weighed heavily upon him. But these nudes, brutal in their frankness, are an important reminder that his sense of outrage on behalf of the poor and the dispossessed, in this case women dispossessed of their individuality, of their bodies, of their sexuality, inspired a series of sharply provocative inventions. Nonetheless, success and fame exacted a price, as Leonardo Sciascia, a fellow Sicilian understood: "The difficulty for Guttuso, for us, for each man born on this island, is to live *after having achieved*, after holding out, not to cave in 'under the load' of riches or glory or simply of those things we have done, things in which we invested and continue to invest our passion. This is Guttuso's struggle, his anguish." [22]

One way of distancing himself from this burden of fame and wealth was to take refuge in what he called 'moments of reflection' ('momenti di pensiero').[23] As he himself recognized, there had always been an element of mystery in his work that 'shunned' ('sfuggiva') the directness of straightforward observation. The example he gives is *The funeral of Togliatti*, but the painting in which his 'moments of reflection' convey a sense of mystery so potent as to evoke the mystery of de Chirico, is not in that heroic spectacle of death, but in the majestically alive 'natura morta' he painted in 1974, *La Vucciria*.

The intensely compressed reality of *La Vucciria*, the name of the street market in the centre of Palermo, is fused with

Guttuso,
Reclining Nude, 1976.
Private collection.

36

an unnatural stillness that locks the image - a gigantic still-life - into a state of dream or reverie. The ordered piles of fresh ripe produce are presented as a joyful and triumphant crowd, more vivid, more alive than the mute human beings who trail through the centre of this abundance. The vitality and generosity that Moravia saw in Guttuso's painting are displayed to the full in what is surely his most eloquent tribute to Sicily. 'Every heap which has human significance has been collected', says Canetti[24] and in *La Vucciria* the sense of 'many hands occupied with picking and harvesting' the rich produce of the Sicilian earth is expressed in an image of simple truth and unforced grandeur. At the same time, the sadness and neglect that are so much a part of Sicily's history, the alienation of the common people from the land, are conveyed through the silent detachment of the figures.

As the earlier work demonstrates so convincingly, it was through the imagery of still-life that Guttuso was best able to express his view of modern Italy. The achievement of *La Vucciria* is the way in which the subject encompasses the past and the present without resorting to the easy rhetoric of history painting. It was presented to the University of Palermo by a close friend of the artist, and it surely fitting that this particular work should be displayed in one of the oldest and most distinguished public spaces in Sicily. It is a reminder of that island's history. It is also a reminder of the responsibility that Guttuso took upon himself - to create an art for the people that would be as persuasive as the billboard, as compelling as the cinema screen, as uplifting as the battle hymn.

1. In his essay, 'L'insegnamento di Picasso', 1953, Guttuso writes about an art which is 'useful' to mankind, and to which people have the same right as they do to 'work, bread and peace'.

2. Douglas Cooper, 'Italian painters of today', *The Listener,* 23 September 1948.

3. On the subject of Guttuso's reputation in Britain from 1945-60, see James Hyman, "A 'Pioneer Painter': Renato Guttuso and Realism in Britain", in this catalogue.

4. *Renato Guttuso: Recent Paintings, Watercolours and Drawings,* Marlborough Fine Art Ltd., London, 1-24 March 1979.

5. James Thrall Soby, catalogue preface in *Renato Guttuso,* Aca-Heller Gallery, New York, 7-28 April 1958; John Berger, catalogue preface in *Renato Guttuso,* The Leicester Galleries, London, March 1955.

6. Richard Wollheim, catalogue preface in

*Guttuso,* McRoberts & Tunnard, London, 23 November-17 December 1960.

7. Alberto Moravia, 'Renato Guttuso' in Franco Grasso, *La vita e l'opera di Guttuso,* Edizione "Il Punto", Palermo, 1962.

8. Ibid.

9. Ibid.

10. Renato Guttuso, 'Paura della Pittura', *Prospettiva,* Rome, no. 25-27, January 1942.

11. Wollheim 1960, op. cit.

12. Renato Guttuso, 'L'insegnamento di Picasso', *La Biennale di Venezia,* 13-14 Alfieri, Venezia, April-June 1953, pp. 58-59.

13. Interview with Guttuso by Ludovico Besozzi, *Playboy,* Milan, November 1980.

14. A. Scotti, *Catalogo dei Manoscritti di Giuseppe Pelizza da Volpedo,* Tortona,

1974, p. 124, given in English translation in the catalogue of *Post-Impressionism: Cross Currents in European Painting,* Royal Academy of Arts, London, 1979-80, p. 246.

15. I am grateful to Fabio Carapezza Guttuso for bringing to my attention the drawings Guttuso made to demonstrate the relation between the *Triumph of Death* and *Guernica.*

16. Renato Guttuso, 'La pittura è il mio mestriere'.

17. I am indebted to Nicholas Dines for allowing me to read his unpublished dissertation, *Antifascist art in fascist space: The example of Renato Guttuso's 'Crucifixion' at the fourth Premio Bergamo of 1942.*

18. Guttuso published an article on Nicolas de Staël in *Il contemporaneo,* October-November 1958.

19. Wollheim 1960, op. cit.

20. Cited in Enrico Crispolti, 'Introduzione

a Guttuso' in *Catalogo ragionato generale dei dipinti di Renato Guttuso* [ed. Enrico Crispolti], vol. 1, Mondadori, Milan, 1983.

21. Moravia describes the women in Guttuso's paintings as follows: 'Love for them is a brief spasm between two bouts of lassitude, a violence unleashed on defenceless and resigned flesh. This love knows all about sheets soaked in sweat, rooms on the outskirts of town, proletarian working class promiscuity. Sometimes about cruelty and violence'. Moravia 1962, op. cit., pp. 16-17.

22. Leonardo Sciascia, 'Guttuso a Palermo', *Corriere della sera,* Milan, 21 January 1971.

23. Luca Liguori, 'Intervista-verità in occasione dell'aperta della mostra di Venezia. Guttuso: in arte la realtà non è socialista', *Il Tempo,* Rome, 4 April 1982 (cited in Crispolti 1983, vol. 1, p. liv).

24. Elias Canetti, *Crowds and Power,* Peregrine Books, 1984, p. 102.

# A "Pioneer Painter":
# Renato Guttuso and Realism in Britain[1]

*James* **Hyman**

*"I know of no young painter at work in Europe today whom I consider more interesting, more talented, more individual or more considerable."*

Douglas Cooper, 1950 [2]

*"Guttuso [is] the most significant painter to have emerged in Europe since the war [...] How we receive his work here [in London] will be a test of our spirit rather than his."*

John Berger, 1955[3]

"Realism today is not a school of painting, nor an involution of taste towards this or that moment in the history of art, but an historical dialectical concept bound to the present [and] strictly connected with modern reality and culture."[4] So declared Renato Guttuso in a high profile debate on realism versus abstraction staged at the Italian Institute in Belgrave Square, London, on 21 March 1955. Making the case for abstraction was the prominent British painter and critic, Patrick Heron.[5] Chairing the event was one of the most respected art historians of the twentieth century, Professor Ernst Gombrich.[6]

Guttuso's lengthy contributions dominated the evening.[7] In a speech that was delivered in Italian and translated by Professor Gombrich, he praised "realist artists [who] pursue the path of democratic art traced by Hogarth, Goya, Delacroix, Courbet, Daumier and Cézanne, on which also appear great and more recent images like Van Gogh's *Chair* or *Guernica*."[8] He identified two evils, "irrationality" and "academic Philistinism", and argued that "the thesis of a renewal of art in the realistic sense necessitates a revision of our recent past."[9] What was needed was "to trace the right main thread, to tie the various small threads together, [to] contribute to the formation of the new destiny of modern art."[10]

The debate encapsulates both the status of Guttuso and the way in which arguments between abstraction and realism dominated British and European art from 1945-60: a feature wittily caricatured in a drawing by Renato Guttuso, *Filofigurativo, antifigurativo*, showing a confused two-faced viewer trying to make sense of the two opposed tendencies. Guttuso's contribution to these British debates had a centrality belied by subsequent neglect. His work was not only known through reproductions - in British publications (such as *Penguin New Writing*, the *Burlington magazine* and *Apollo*) and imported journals (especially *Realismo*) - but was also transmitted through one-person shows and group exhibitions in London. Guttuso also established friendships with many British artists, critics and curators through their visits to Italy and his to London.

As early as 1947 the Redfern Gallery staged *Contemporary Italian Art* which included Guttuso. Then in 1948 Guttuso's paintings at the Venice Biennale attracted enthusiastic responses from leading British critics including Herbert Read and Douglas Cooper and shortly thereafter *Penguin New Writing*, which along with *Horizon* was the most important cultural journal of the decade, published an essay on Guttuso by John Fleming.[11] For Fleming,

Photograph: Guttuso, Patrick Heron and Prof. Gombrich at the realism versus abstraction debate, Italian Institute, London 1955.

Guttuso's particular importance was formal and lay in the way "he has understood and assimilated the problems of the cubists and post-cubist painting."[12] Fleming did not include any reference to the artist's politics but characterized Guttuso's figures as "elemental beings who toil and sweat to earn a hard living by the strength of their bodies."[13] This message was reinforced by the choice of accompanying illustrations which, given the lack of knowledge about Guttuso's political activities, implied affinities between Guttuso and young British artists whose own social concerns were far removed from the Italian's agenda. Alongside three heavily stylized works by Guttuso - *Melon Eaters* (1946), *Seamstresses* (1947) and *Still Life* (1947) - the reproductions included Michael Ayrton's *Thames Foreshore* and *Broken Seawall* and Prunella Clough's *Fisherman with Skate* (1946). All were interested in prosaic genre scenes, manual labour or artisan trade.

This provided the context for Guttuso's first one-person show in London in 1950. This took place at the instigation of Douglas Cooper and was held at the most important showcase for international avant garde art in London, Erica Brausen's Hanover Gallery.[14] In the catalogue Cooper's claims could not have been higher as he praised "one of the first young painters in whose work modern art comes nearer, once again, to life."[15] The impression that it gave of Guttuso was, however, extremely partial. Indeed both the selection of images for *Penguin New Writing* and the presentation of pictures at the Redfern and Hanover galleries conspicuously omitted Guttuso's more political work, consisting mainly of landscapes and still lifes.

Guttuso: Filofigurativo, antifigurativo, drawing, 1950. Private collection.

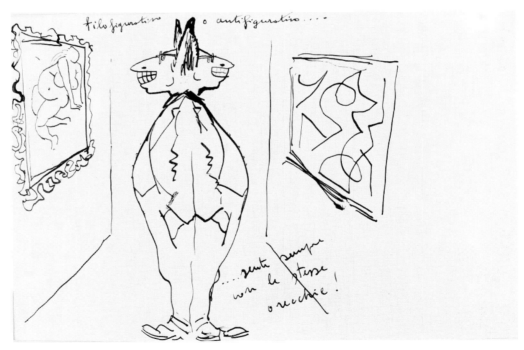

This perception would change by the mid 1950s as British knowledge increased concerning the political context for Guttuso's work. In 1955 a generally well received exhibition of recent work by Guttuso was held at the Leicester Galleries.[16] Then in 1956 the same gallery held an exhibition of young Italian realists, presenting Guttuso and many of his colleagues. The year ended with a Tate Gallery showing of an Arts Council touring exhibition, *Modern Italian Art from the Estorick Collection*, a survey show which included work by Guttuso.[17]

Such visibility ensured that by the mid 1950s Guttuso had become a litmus test for the leading British critics: a focus for responses to realism. Attitudes were polarized between eulogy and condemnation. As John Berger observed at the time, Guttuso's 1955 exhibition "provoked, infuriated or inspired those who saw it."[18]

For promoters of modernism, formalism and abstraction, and critics of social or socialist realism Guttuso served as a focus for their opposition. For Patrick Heron, the prominent young painter-critic; David Sylvester, the curator, lecturer and art critic; and Lawrence Gowing, the painter, writer and teacher, Guttuso was to be condemned, his abilities as a painter questioned and his politics rejected.

David Sylvester was one of the earliest British critics of Guttuso. In 1950, having recognized the significance of Cooper's support, he nonetheless judged Guttuso to be "an artistic failure".[19] Then in 1955 he used his review of the

Melon Eaters (*oil*—1946)

RENATO GUTTUSO

Seamstresses (*oil*—1947)

Guttuso: illustrations from Penguin New Writing: Melon Eaters (1946), Seamstresses (1947) and Still Life (1947).

RENATO GUTTUSO

Still Life (*oil*—1947)

Italian's London show to make explicit the political implications that underlay aesthetic criticism. Acclaim for Guttuso, suggested Sylvester, "must be due to the anxiety of western communists to find *anyone* whose painting suits the party line without being palpably philistine [...] he has the gift for operatic oversimplifying of the human situation which is possessed by all effective communist propagandists."[20] This view was reinforced by Lawrence Gowing, a former member of the Communist Party who had rejected its ideology. Describing Guttuso as "anti-human", Gowing questioned his attitude to violence and challenged his assumed "sympathy for victims."[21] What Gowing identified was not Guttuso's identification with his subjects but ambiguity: "the ambiguity of Guttuso"s standpoint is, at root, exactly that equivocation which convicts Communism of treachery to the human values for which it speaks."[22]

But for those on the far left, Guttuso was a beacon of hope. Initially, in mid 1950, Derek Chittock, a Communist and AIA activist, was an almost lone voice in praising Guttuso's political activism. His review of Guttuso's 1950 exhibition made claims for the Italian's socialist realism and welcomed the visit of a "pioneer painter of Italy" and "an outstanding representative of a great new movement in Italy."[23] This response, however, owed more to the writer's own knowledge of European realism than it did to what he would have learned from Guttuso's presentation in London. But later that year Guttuso's involvement with the Sheffield Peace Conference decisively helped establish

Michael Ayrton, The Captive Seven, exhibited in Sixty for '51, Festival of Britain, London, 1951. Tate Gallery, London.

the Italian's reputation amongst those of the left in Britain. Just a few months after Guttuso had visited London for his Hanover Gallery exhibition, he sought to reenter Britain as a delegate for the Peace Conference. But he was one of the many Communist intellectuals to be refused entry. This received publicity when Guttuso's angry letter to Sir Victor Mallet, the British Ambassador in Rome, was leaked to the press. In it Guttuso wrote that "these men whom you declared to be unwanted were not setting out to undermine the fortunes of the English nation. They were coming to England to affirm the right of peoples to live in peace and to invite governments to discussion without having recourse to arms."[24]

This controversy ensured that although little was known of either Guttuso's activities for the Italian Communist Party or of his political paintings, from now on Guttuso would be known in Britain for both his politics and his painting. Now Guttuso began to be taken up by British champions from the far left who made increasing reference to a subject which previous supporters such as Cooper had politely avoided: Guttuso's politics. Particularly vocal were John Berger and Benedict Nicholson who first met in 1951 and whose subsequent promotion of Guttuso was a joint project.[25]

This shift in appreciation reached its apotheosis with Guttuso's second one – person exhibition in London which took place at the Leicester Galleries in 1955.[26] Now it was not Douglas Cooper, but John Berger, who wrote the catalogue

Guttuso,
Spaghetti Eater,
illustration from Elizabeth David's
Italian Food.

preface and now it was the social function of Guttuso's art that was celebrated. As Berger argued: "sustained by a binding faith in his fellow men, he [Guttuso] has always understood that the artist's responsibility in not only to what his brush does to his canvas, but also for what his canvas does to those who gaze at it."[27]

This message was reinforced the following year with the Leicester Galleries' group exhibition of Italian realism. This not only presented barely known Italian realists to a British public but also socially and politically contextualized Guttuso through its selection of ten Italian artists associated both with the "La Colonna" Gallery in Milan and with the Communist broadsheet *Realismo*: Bueno, Francese, Guttuso, Migneco, Mucchi, Pizzinato, Rossi, Sassu, Treccani and Zigaina. The catalogue once again included an introductory essay by John Berger and complemented this with biographical notes on each artist which emphasized the links between art practice and political activism: "Italian artists and intellectuals", wrote Berger, "realise that they can be nothing unless they are the spokesmen of the people."[28]
Berger's enthusiasm reached its peak with a vivid essay on *La Spiaggia* for the final issue of a short-lived and little-known publication, *Realism*, which was run by the Artists Group of the Communist Party of Great Britain (CPGB).[29] This prize winning picture from the Venice Biennale of 1956 was according to Berger "Guttuso's greatest painting" in large part because of its subject matter: "it requires very much more imagination to make a scene of pleasure heroic than a scene of conflict or labour."[30] It filled a "vacuum in bourgeois culture caused by the total

John Minton: illustration from Elizabeth David's A book of Mediterranean Food.

inability of the bourgeoisie to create or even conceive of contemporary heroic characters". Unlike images of 'Pin-Up' girls and commercial 'lies', Guttuso realised a new 'truth' and provided "an expression of *joie de vivre*."[31]

Appropriately such praise led Berger to Italy where he stayed with Guttuso, writing a monograph on the artist which was published in 1957.[32] He also used a rare contribution to a foreign publication, for the Italian journal *Rinascita*, to make his most direct comparisons between the the scarcity of social realism in Britain and the flourishing humanism of the Italian realists.[33] In a lengthy essay, "La Pittura inglese di fronte a Guttuso", Berger adopted a strategy reminiscent of Guttuso's contribution to the Italian Institute debate just a few weeks earlier, locating realism at the end of a tradition. He constructed an English path from William Hogarth and eighteenth-century caricature through nineteenth-century illustrators to the present continuation of an English graphic and illustrative tradition. As contemporary practitioners Berger cited two artists associated with the Artists Group of the Communist Party of Great Britain. He praised Paul Hogarth for his 'reportage' drawings made on his travels in Europe and championed Clifford Rowe, who had recently completed murals for the ETU, depicting the history of the British labour movement.[34]

However, despite Berger's admission that the situation in Britain - typified by the reputation of the 'anti-humanist' individualism of Francis Bacon - was far removed from the more affirmative, collective spirit of Guttuso and his compatriots, the art of Italy ranging from the painting of Guttuso to the sculpture of Marino Marini and the cinema

Guttuso,
Battle of Ponte
dell'Ammiraglio, 1950-51.
Private collection.

of the Italian realists did have an impact on many British artists, especially during the late 1940s and early 1950s. This impact has, however, been obscured by the dominance of first French and then American culture.

Guttuso himself made many friendships with British artists. In 1950 when he visited London for his Hanover Gallery exhibition he was, in his own words, "fraternally received by English friends and colleagues."[35] One party was held by Derek Kartun, the foreign editor of the *Daily Worker*, where the guests included members of the Artists International Association among them Barbara Niven and members and former members of the Communist Party of Great Britain, such as the writer Raymond Watkinson and the artist Harry Baines.[36] Others Guttuso met on this visit included Henry Moore and Roland Penrose who had both shown support for Communism, Graham Sutherland, Derek Hill and Bernard Berenson.[37] These meetings were strengthened by correspondence, visits by British artists and critics to Italy and Guttuso's return visit to London in 1955.[38] A subsequent party was held by the architect, Erno Goldfinger, at his home in Hampstead. George Weidenfeld, the publisher, became a friend[39]; Kenneth Clark, Director of the National Gallery, held a party for Guttuso at the Arts Council where the guests included Henry Moore[40]; and Derrick Greaves, the young English social realist, held a party where the young artists present included George Fullard, Edward Middleditch, Leslie Duxbury and Alfred Daniels;[41] and Richard Wollheim, one of the artist's closest English friends, was also responsible for arranging for Guttuso to visit the Slade School of Art to judge a prize.[42]

John Minton,
The Death of Nelson, 1952 .

British ties with Italy were not confined to those interested in social realism. Amongst older artists, two artists of the left, Michael Ayrton and John Minton, both echoed Guttuso.[43] Rome scholarships allowed students including Derrick Greaves and Michael Andrews to study in Italy; and unpublished letters from Francis Bacon to his dealer, Erica Brausen, reveal that while living in Italy in 1954, he tried to find a studio in Rome.[44] Despite the anti-modernist, isolationist rhetoric of Ayrton's writing, his paintings owe much to aspects of the formal language of his *bête noire*, Pablo Picasso, as mediated by the example of Guttuso. This is especially evident in the late 1940s and early 1950s when Ayrton traveled in Italy. In 1950, the year Guttuso showed in London, Ayrton even exhibited at the Italian's gallery, Galleria del Milione, in Milan, a centre for Italian realism.[45] This coincided with one of the most important and most public projects of Ayrton's career: his contribution to the Festival of Britain exhibition *Sixty Paintings for 51*. In one of the largest paintings he had attempted, *The Captive Seven* (1949-50), Ayrton showed a scene that had strong affinities with Guttuso in scale and ambition: a highly stylized image of poverty-stricken people in a street in Trastevere, a poor quarter of Rome.

John Minton, meanwhile, not only paralleled Guttuso as an illustrator, draughtsman and lithographer, but as a painter. In 1952 Minton produced one of his most ambitious paintings, *The Death of Nelson* (1952), in which the scale, multi-figure composition, right to left thrust and scattering of fallen figures echo Guttuso's *Battaglia di Ponte dell'Ammiraglio* (1951-52).[46] Then in 1954 Guttuso illustrated Elizabeth David's *Italian Food* (Macdonald, London 1954), producing drawings which included a man eating pasta and a series of table-top still lifes of wine bottles, fish, fruit and vegetables.[47] The following year Minton produced drawings of a similar style as well as content for Elizabeth David's *A book of Mediterranean Food*.

The impact of Guttuso on British painters is, however, most direct in the work of two artists who shared the Italian's political position, the muralist, illustrator and draughtsman, Harry Baines, and the painter and critic, Peter de Francia, both of whom became friends with Guttuso in the late 1940s and early 1950s.[48] Baines's portfolio of lithographs, *Quarrymen* (1953), is almost unprecedented in British art of the period and contains not only echoes of Van Gogh's heavy use of line and Courbet's depiction of labourers but also, more immediately, Guttuso's paintings of this subject from the late 1940s and early 1950s such as *Carrello in miniera* (1949), which was owned by Douglas Cooper, and *Picconiere di Bagheria* (1952).[49]

Peter de Francia, unlike most British artists and writers, was also deeply aware of the political situation in Italy during the mid 1950s, talking at length with Guttuso not only in the late 1940s but also at the time he was painting *La Spiaggia* (1955-56).[50] Peter de Francia also read two of the journals for which Guttuso wrote, *Realismo* and *Il Contemporaneo*, whose editor was a close friend.[51] *The Bombing of Sakiet* (1958), de Francia's major painting of the 1950s - a response to a bombing raid by the French airforce on the Tunisian-Algerian border - was a rare example of an artist working in Britain attempting the type of epic Socialist Realist painting encouraged by the example of Guttuso, echoing the Italian's *Flight from Etna during an Eruption* (1938).

Another young artist, Derrick Greaves, met Guttuso in Italy in 1953 and the impact of this meeting was soon evident in his paintings, such as the monumental *Sicilian Subject*, which was exhibited at the Venice Biennale in 1956.[52] The rough texture, humble subject-matter and sun-baked colours not only reflect Greaves's admiration for paintings on the sides of Italian carts used by the agricultural workers which he saw when he visited Guttuso's birthplace, Bagheria but also echo paintings by the Italian such as *Carrettiere Siciliano Addormentato* (1946).[53]

However, as such examples indicate, British responses to Guttuso were extremely variable, rarely introducing overtly political subjects. This in many ways reflected Guttuso's own self-presentation in London, characterized by his contribution to the Italian Institute debate of 1955. Speaking then, Guttuso had taken care to present his case for realism to a London audience by veiling its political implications, making no direct reference to social or socialist realism. Strategically, this divorcing of aesthetic and political claims was astute, for the mid 1950s was a time in which Western promotion of culture was dominated by a vigorous promotion of the idea that art could and necessarily should be free from outside influence. A stress on artistic freedom and an emphasis on individual vision coexisted with criticism of the idea that art and life should be inseparably linked. Rather, art was concerned with creating a new world. Its territory was separate and distinct.

Harry Baines,
lithograph from Quarrymen,
Portfolio, Berkeley Galleries,
London 1953

Guttuso stood against this. For him and his allies art had a social function and a practical use. Realism was not a question of personal aesthetic choice. It reflected an ideological position and implied a specific political orientation. In London Guttuso addressed this relationship with subtlety; polite British supporters such as Cooper and Read hardly at all; and bold champions from the left such as de Francia and Berger with vigour. The result was that by the mid 1950s - at the height of the Cold War - Marxist claims for Guttuso as a political artist had drowned out more establishment praise for his aesthetic abilities. As the identification of Guttuso with Communism grew in Britain, so his position became more marginal. A number of factors accentuated this: a lengthy Conservative administration; the lack of a strong Communist movement as in Italy; and the decimation of CPGB support after Soviet intervention in Hungary in 1956. Despite his growing maturity as an artist, Guttuso would never again assume the prominence in Britain that he had achieved at the beginning and middle of the 1950s.

It is only now, four decades later, that this neglect is being redressed and, significantly, this belated reappraisal has come, less through an appreciation of Guttuso's aims as a propagandist, than through a recognition of his abilities as a painter. Appreciation of Guttuso has come full circle. In the 1940s it was still-lifes and genre scenes that introduced Guttuso to a British public. Half a century later, such works once again form a basis for British appreciation of the vitality of Renato Guttuso.

Peter de Francia,
The Bombing of Sakiet, 1958 .

1   This essay is dedicated to the memory of Harry Baines (1910-1995). I would like to thank the following for their help: the late Harry Baines, Pauline Baines, Peter de Francia, Sir Ernst Gombrich, Derrick Greaves, Paul Hogarth, Derek Kartun, David Sylvester, Raymond Watkinson and Richard Wollheim. At the Courtauld Institute I am grateful to Margaret Garlake for reading the manuscript and Andrew Wilson for information on Patrick Heron. Particular thanks are due to Fabio Carapezza Guttuso at the Archivi Guttuso, Roma, for providing unpublished correspondence between Guttuso and British artists and writers.

2   Douglas Cooper, "Preface", *Renato Guttuso/Catherine Yarrow*, Hanover Gallery, London, 1 June-1 July 1950.

3   John Berger, "Preface", *Renato Guttuso*, Leicester Galleries, London, 1955.

4   Renato Guttuso, from an English language typescript, London 1955. I am grateful to Harry Baines for informing me of this debate and for supplying a typescript of this previously unpublished speech given to him by the artist. Interview with Harry Baines, 11 March 1994.

5   Heron's impressions of the event are indicated by two letters of 23 May 1955. He wrote to Guttuso that "there is much interest over here in the issues which we discussed", adding that the journal "*Twentieth Century*" is anxious to publish both our speeches in its issue in July." Heron concluded: "I much enjoyed meeting you in London. I only wish we could have had longer to talk about the matters that divide us - and in the same language! We were handicapped in this." Patrick Heron, letter to Renato Guttuso, 23 May 1955. Archivi Guttuso. The proposed publication of Guttuso's text never took place. That same day Heron also wrote a triumphalist letter to the American modernist critic, Clement Greenberg, about the success of his own contribution to the debate in undermining Guttuso's claims for realism. Patrick Heron, letter to Clement Greenberg, 23 May 1955, Clement Greenberg papers, Archives of American Art, Smithsonian Library, Washington, D.C. I am grateful to the Heron specialist, Andrew Wilson, for informing me of this letter to Greenberg and another letter, to Sir Herbert Read, in which Heron wrote "Guttuso v. charming: but I don't think I trust him. Member of Central Committee of the Italian Communist Party." Patrick Heron, letter to Sir Herbert Read, 25 March 1955. University of Victoria, British Caledonia, Special Collections.

6   Recalling the event, Professor Gombrich suggested that Guttuso was a "skilful politician" who, despite speaking in Italian, was a "vigorous and articulate combatant" who made his case more persuasively than Patrick Heron who was less experienced at public speaking. Conversation with Sir Ernst Gombrich, 17 June 1994.

7   Heron gives an indication of the length of Guttuso's contribution in a letter written shortly after the event: Guttuso, he wrote, "expanded the prepared 20 minutes script of his speech [...] into a 45 minute one [and] he also wrote a second 25 minute speech *in answer* to mine [...] Finally, discussion from the audience was disallowed! Guttuso = 45 + 25 = 70 minutes in Italian. Heron = 20 + 10 = 30 minutes in English. A Communist idea of a fair discussion!" Heron to Read op. cit.

8   op. cit.

9   ibid.

10  ibid.

11  Herbert Read illustrated Guttuso's *The Beach* (1946) in his reissued *Art Now*, Faber and Faber, London (revised and enlarged edition, 1948). However, the artist is not referred to in the text. For Cooper's response to Guttuso see: Douglas Cooper, "Italian Painting of Today", *Listener*, London, 13 September 1948. Cooper first saw pictures by Guttuso in Rome in 1945. On this see Douglas Cooper, untitled essay in *Omaggio a Guttuso*, Il Nuovo Piccolo, supplemento al n.1, 1964. Richard Wollheim believes that Cooper met Guttuso through Picasso who was a great admirer of the Italian. Picasso himself met Guttuso in 1946. Wollheim, letter to the author, 5 April 1996. Letters in the Archivi Guttuso show that Cooper and Guttuso had began corresponding by early 1947. Cooper's knowledge of Italian art and admiration for Guttuso is evident in his proposal to Guttuso for an exhibition of 5 Italian artists: Boccioni, Morandi, De Pisis, Campigli and Guttuso. Douglas Cooper, letter to Guttuso, 31 January 1948. Archivi Guttuso. See also John Fleming, "A note on Renato Guttuso", *Penguin New Writing*, London, no. 34, 1948, pp.124-125.

12  ibid.

13  ibid.

14  Correspondence between Cooper and Guttuso from early 1950 includes Cooper's proposal for an exhibition at the Hanover Gallery. In one of these letters (written from London in French) Cooper wrote that he was still waiting to hear if Guttuso wished to exhibit, enclosed a plan of the gallery space and proposed that the paintings selected should arrive in London by 15 May 1950. Subsequent letters contained details of the planned selection. Archivi Guttuso. Cooper was also already a collector of Guttuso, lending two pictures to the Hanover Gallery show.

Guttuso,
The Beach, 1956.

15 "Preface", op. cit. Exhibition reviews and purchases show that the exhibition was generally well received. For details see the sales ledgers and press cuttings files of the Hanover Gallery, Tate Gallery Archive, London. Sales ledgers coinciding with the 1950 show include the purchase by the Tate Gallery of two watercolours: *Campieri* (1949) which showed men on horseback; and *Sulphur Miners* (1949). However, neither of these works is listed in the 1950 exhibition catalogue.

16 John Berger,"Preface", *Realist Painters of 'La Colonna'*, Leicester Galleries, London, 9-31 May 1956. Simultaneously, in another room of the Leicester Galleries there was an exhibition by the former Euston Road painter, Rodrigo Moynihan. A number of reviewers contrasted the reserved figuration of the Englishman with the energetic realism of the Italian. See especially David Sylvester, "Renato Guttuso and Rodrigo Moynihan", *The Listener*, 17 March 1955, p.486; John Russell, "Eminences", *Sunday Times*, 13 March 1955; and Nevile Wallis, "At the Galleries", *The Observer*, 13 March 1955.

17 The tour began at the Tate Gallery in November-December 1956.

18 John Berger, "La Colonna", op. cit.

19 Sylvester argued that "a great deal of force has gone into the painting, but little of it comes out in expression.

Figures are shown in movement only they don't move [...] Guttuso's work fails to function plastically and dynamically. His simplification and distortions are banal [...] a great deal of power is displayed in them, but it isn't put to any purpose." David Sylvester, "Guttuso and Catherine Yarrow", *Art News and Review*, 17 June 1950, vol.2, no. 10, p. 5.

20 Admitting that Guttuso was "a good journalist in paint", Sylvester praised his "small, sketchy" pictures but questioned whether he was equipped for bolder ambitions. Sylvester, "Renato Guttuso and Rodrigo Moynihan". op. cit.

21 Lawrence Gowing, "Letter to the Editor", *New Statesman*, 2 April 1955, vol. 49, no. 1256, p. 474.

22 ibid.

23 Derek Chittock, "A Pioneer Painter of Italy", *Daily Worker*, 13 June 1950.

24 As quoted in *The Manchester Guardian*, op. cit.

25 The two critics were introduced to each other in 1951 by David Sylvester. Conversation with David Sylvester op. cit. See especially: John Berger, "A Social Realist Painting at the Biennale", *Burlington*, October 1952, Vol. XCIV, no. 595, pp. 294-295; and John Berger, "Guttuso: A Conversation", *New Statesman*, 19 March 1955, vol.

49, no. 1254, p. 384. (Although listed under Berger in the index of the *New Statesman* this text was a discussion between Berger and Benedict Nicholson.)

26 *Renato Guttuso*, Leicester Galleries, London, March 1955. The catalogue lists 20 pictures, all from 1952-54, including *Calabrian Village*, *Portrait of a Sicilian Miner*, *Woman Carrying Washing*, *Killed Warrior*, *The Shooting of Patriots* and *Boogie-Woogie in Rome*.

27 John Berger, "Preface", *Renato Guttuso*, Leicester Galleries, London, March 1955.

28 John Berger, *"La Colonna"*, op. cit.

29 John Berger, "The Beach", *Realism*, November-December 1956, no. 6, p. 3.

30 ibid.

31 ibid.

32 There was no English or English language edition of Berger's monograph: John Berger, *Guttuso*, Verlag der Kunst, Dresden, East Germany, 1957.

33 John Berger, "La Pittura inglese di fronte a Guttuso", *Rinascita*, no. 5, Roma, Maggio, 1955, pp. 375-377. Criticising British artists for avoiding subjects such as Hiroshima and the

bomb, Berger explained that "la drammatica influenza della mostra di Guttuso a Londra" was because "alla pittura inglese è stato presentato un artista veramente contemporaneo, pieno di immaginazione, che osa rischiare e sa comunicare invece di alludere." ibid.

34 See especially Hogarth's publications of the early 1950s such as *Defiant People: Drawings of Greece Today* (intro. James Aldridge), Lawrence and Wishart, London, 1953; and *Looking at China with the journal of the artist*, Lawrence and Wishart, London, 1956. Both books may be considered distant cousins of Guttuso's wartime *Gott Mirr Uns* drawings which Hogarth admired. For information on Hogarth's reportage see *Paul Hogarth: Cold War Reports, 1947-67*, The Norwich Gallery, Norfolk Institute of Art and Design, Norfolk, 1990. For information on Clifford Rowe see R.W. Watkinson, "Introduction", *Fighting Spirits: Peter Peri and Clifford Rowe*, Journeyman/Camden Art Centre, London, 1987.

35 Guttuso, as quoted in an unsigned review, "An Italian Protest on Sheffield", *Manchester Guardian*, 22 November 1950. Hanover Archive.

36 Kartun met Guttuso on this visit, but had no real relationship with the artist, simply allowing his house to be used for the party. Conversation with Derek Kartun, 12 January 1996.

Installation photography
of the exhibition
Four Young Painters,
British Pavilion,
Venice Biennale, 1956.
On the far wall is Sicilian
Subject by Derrick Greaves.
[photo: courtesy
of the Mayor Gallery]

37  Evidence of ongoing friendships is contained in the Archivi Guttuso. Graham Sutherland, for example, wrote that he "saw and admired works of yours in the Biennale at Venice" and discussed a planned trip to Italy. Graham Sutherland, letter to Renato Guttuso, 11 March 1951. Archivi Guttuso.

38  Sir Herbert Read, for example, wrote thanking Guttuso and his wife for "the *MAGICAL* evening you gave us. It all seems like a dream now, in this distant countryside where the snow is still on the hills and the sun, alas, rarely shines." Herbert Read, postcard to Renato Guttuso, postmarked 14 May 1955. Archivi Guttuso.

39  See George Weidenfeld, *Remembering My Good Friends*, Harper Collins, London, 1995.

40  The Arts Council party is referred to in a letter from Henry Moore to Renato Guttuso dated 12 April 1955. Archivi Guttuso.

41  Derrick Greaves, letter to the author, 8 February 1994.

42  This visit was arranged by the writer and philosopher Richard Wollheim. It was requested by two students with far left sympathies, Mario Dubsky and Patrick Prockter. Wollheim, letter to the author, 5 april 1996.
Wollheim met Guttuso through Dou-

glas Cooper and was one of the artist's closest British friends during the period 1952-66. The two men had an active correspondence, including a long letter from Guttuso about the notorious Russian invasion of Hungary in 1956. Wollheim also stayed with Guttuso in Velate several times, including one visit during which they drove together to Amsterdam to see the Rembrandt exhibition, stopping en route to see the Isenheim altarpiece in Colmar. Wollheim was also instrumental in the Tate's purchase of *La Discussione*.

43  Ayrton's mother, Barbara Ayrton Gould, was a prominent Labour Member of Parliament and a one time Chairman of the Party. Minton's sympathies are illustrated by his contributions in the mid 1940s to *Our Time*, a small independent political and cultural journal that was, nonetheless, linked to the Communist Party of Great Britain.

44  Francis Bacon, unpublished letters to Erica Brausen. Hanover Archive.

45  *Dipinti e disegni di Michael Ayrton*, Galleria del Milione, Milan, April 1950.

46  I am grateful to David Sylvester for suggesting this comparison. Conversation, 30 December 1995. In fact Minton may well have known Guttuso's battle scene through reproduction. It was the subject of an article by John Berger, which was accompanied by photographs of the

whole picture and close up details: John Berger, *Burlington*, op. cit.

47  The acknowledgements reveal that the idea for the book came from John Lehmann, the editor of *Penguin New Writing*. This connection may explain the choice of Guttuso as illustrator.

48  Harry Baines was a prewar mural painter, a postwar AIA activist and a sometime Communist Party member. Over 1950-51 he traveled in Europe, met Renato Guttuso and returned to London with portfolios of lithographs by Italian and French socialist realists which were unavailable in Britain. Peter de Francia worked with Guttuso in Italy as early as 1947 and returned two years later to spend most of 1949 working alongside him. He exhibited twice in Milan.

49  Baines's *Quarrymen* portfolio was published to coincide with the artist's one-person exhibition at the Berkeley Gallery, London in 1953. It included a text by John Berger.

50  Peter de Francia recalls that the extent of British knowledge of Guttuso's political activities was 'almost nil', suggesting that exceptions included the historian and sociologist Eric Hobsbawm; Stuart Hood and Basil Davidson who had been close to the Italian Resistance during 1942-45; Wogan Philips (Lord Milford), Harry Baines and John Berger. Peter de

Francia, letter to the author, 7 January 1996. In 1952 de Francia sought to increase British knowledge of Guttuso by bringing to London the large version of *Operaio morto* for a group exhibition sponsored in part by Guttuso, for the Artists for Peace group.

51  Peter de Francia, letter to the author, 8 February 1994. See also Peter de Francia, "Renato Guttuso", *Art Monthly*, March 1987, no.104, pp. 20-22. This obituary contrasts Guttuso's low status in Britain with wide-spread acclaim in the Communist world. It notes that when Guttuso died, Soviet President Mikhail Gorbachev was among those who sent condolences.

52  This Italian influence was identified and praised by Berger who frequently championed young British realists by celebrating their relationship to Italian realism. See, for example, John Berger, "Greaves and [Paul] Hogarth", *New Statesman*, London, 10 December 1955, vol.50, no.1292, p.792. Berger wrote of the paintings of Greaves: "their subject matter, their light and colour, are all Italian, their under-statement and bound-in passions are very English [...] Greaves is no longer promising: he is, whether recognized or not, a European artist."

53  Greaves, himself, recognizes affinities with Guttuso "in both colour and presentation of narrative." letter from Derrick Greaves, 4 March 1994.

Clifford Rowe,
ETU Mural, 1954.

# Italians, Tell Your Story
# Guttuso among the men of letters

*Massimo* **Onofri**

Anyone wishing to undertake an overall examination of the imposing and diverse, let us even say monumental achievement of Renato Guttuso, with a view not only to a history of twentieth-century art but to one which could evolve into a wider and more articulated history of culture, could not fail to ask for what mysterious reasons this body of work, in an era of unprecedented change, has consistently met with a consensus of approval among men of letters. This is a fate which, in our century, in Italy, perhaps has befallen only Fabrizio Clerici – that Clerici who, however, according to a judgment which has now become axiomatic, was too skilled and genially self-satisfied as a draughtsman not to meet with the icy indifference of professional art historians: those enthusiastic supporters of artistic progress of whatever nature, provided it was founded on a contempt for drawing and painting, and who, to conclude, are used to measuring the beauty of a work of art sometimes in the name of a pre-established poetics, often pursued with engineer-like obstinacy, in terms of its presumed capacity to transgress a consolidated norm.

These are idiots of the most varied kinds, given at times to the odd flash of imbecility, who did not spare Guttuso. But, because of the medals won on the field of a revolution, not just formal in character, the painter succeeded in neutralising their criticism. Not least, he experienced, at first hand and in advance of others, the great adventure of the European *avant-garde* that had as its starting point Picasso. However, coming back to the question that most interests us: why, then, did Guttuso enjoy such favour with writers and poets, whose work often mirrored his own? Writers and poets, it should be noted, whose names embody much of the best in Italian culture over the last fifty years: Corrado Alvaro, Libero De Libero, Elio Vittorini, Guido Piovene, Mario Soldati, Alberto Moravia, Elsa Morante, Carlo Levi, Natalino Sapegno, Gianfranco Contini, Pier Paolo Pasolini, Leonardo Sciascia, Goffredo Parise, Alberto Arbasino, Giovanni Testori, Enzo Siciliano, Vincenzo Consolo, to name just a few.

At this point, leaving aside the fact that Guttuso was also a very shrewd critic and a vigorous writer, a first possible answer, strong enough to begin the discussion, can be found in a statement made by Moravia when introducing an exhibition of Guttuso's paintings at a gallery in Genoa. He described *Fucilazione in campagna* (Execution in the country), 1938, as "more in the manner of Goya than of Manet", displaying "a certain brief, epigrammatic, dramatic quality", which might one day have been developed and articulated "into true composition paintings". It was that brief, epigrammatic and dramatic quality that had induced Vittorini to translate the painter's powerful empathy for popular traditions into true gifts for "description" and "narration". This happened regardless of the fact that such a gift might vary in form "from mimetic sign to rhetorical gesture", "from naturalistic precision to theatrical agitation".

Here we come to the real point: the pictures that Guttuso was painting at the end of the 1930s, in petty and hypocritical Italy, opened up wide onto a tragic and new world, while seemingly reshaping it within an unusual and dramatic narrative sequence. Or rather: the geometrical composition of those pictures opened them up to narration. They presupposed and prefigured narration, so that the syntax of space was resolved in the sense, sometimes even the idea, of time. Within this perspective, Guttuso seemed to be moving in the opposite direction to Morandi, almost rekindling through a narration centred around objects, and making use of objects, what had been implacably extinguished. In the process he recovered, from the outset, the dramatic, perhaps dramaturgic, quality of the existence of these very objects in the world. Italian painting, which had aimed at the same expressive intensity as had been present in the early poetry of Ungaretti and Montale, now discovered the temptation of novelistic form.

Assuming the above to be true, it is perhaps not impossible to provide an interpretation of Guttuso's work running parallel to that of Italian literary history in the same period, in order to verify whether and to what extent this work was able to respond to promptings coming from events which transcended the world of painting. This is a line of investigation which, if proved positive, would give us a reasonably approximate, if not rigorously accurate, answer to our question. Still, there should be no misunderstanding: no one should believe that it is really possible to understand work which is at once so rich, so multi-layered, and so erudite in its play on the complicated rhetorics of quotation, without first taking into account all the subtle genealogies which led to the creation of a particular picture, at a precise historical moment. How could one talk about Guttuso without naming Rembrandt, Goya, David, Géricault, Courbet, Van Gogh, Cézanne, Carrà, Morandi, Picasso, Mondrian and so many others? However, the fact remains that reading Guttuso's paintings as if they were books about the Italy that once was, will perhaps help us to understand why so many writers saw in him the painter who had succeeded in articulating their dismay. Returning to *Execution in the country,* it is Guttuso himself, speaking of this painting, who provides us with a possible lead, to help us develop our argument further: "In Milan I met Vittorini and for two seasons we lived in the same little Bocca di Magra *pensione*: at that time, he was a courier for the Italian Communist Party. He travelled all over Italy with a suitcase full of manifestoes and clandestine newspapers, while writing *Conversazione in Sicilia* (A Conversation in Sicily). It was in the wake of that revolutionary book, and as an echo to its title, that I painted my *Execution in the country*, dedicated to the memory of Garcia Lorca". Hence the association with Vittorini and his novel, published in instalments in 1938-39 by the celebrated review *Letteratura*, a novel that is feverish and stupefying for the abundant sense of amazed and obstinate revolt that it provoked.

What was it about that *Conversazione* that was so urgent and burning as to overwhelm a painter like Guttuso, already mature and recognizable? There was, first of all, the discovery of a "violated society" which tallied with the Sicily in which Guttuso was also born, with its generations of social immobility, and which had hitherto known, as Maurizio Calvesi puts it, only "the rape of sun and blood". Then, there was the clear presentiment that the novel constituted "an epic of liberty" as Geno Pampaloni was to define it. Above all, the rhythm of the final part took on an almost biblical, hieratic quality. Lastly, it had the seductive charm of a prose which at times bubbled over into expressionism. However, it must be said that in the pressing urgency of *Conversazione* Guttuso would certainly not have found the lyrical will to imprint, within such an image of Sicily, every historical and anthropological determination. In this sense, Vittorini's work was only the intermediate stage in a Sicilian journey whose terminus coincided precisely with that of Giovanni Verga. The painting which followed, *Fuga dall'Etna* (Flight from Etna), 1938-9, is the extravagant confirmation of this.

In order to understand the breadth of the contribution from Verga, and what it may have meant in the story of Guttuso, we must mention the prestige that the author of *I Malavoglia* was reacquiring, after a long eclipse, in Italian culture of the period. This revival, leaving aside the isolated and not always perspicacious essay that Croce wrote in 1903, was due above all to the book that Luigi Russo completed in May 1919. This book sought the reasons for so much misunderstanding and for the first time re-examined the writer's whole literary story, measuring the meaning of and reasons for the experience of *verismo* in relation to the youthful novels. It reconstructed the moral world of the works

Guttuso,
The Occupation of land, 1947.
Szépmüvészeti Múzeum, Budapest.

and, in Croce's wake, defined, without any further uncertainty their poetry and informing sentiments. In the process, it freed the terrain from so many false critical problems and elevated Verga's works, definitively and beyond all doubt, in the academic sphere, to the status of classics.

Soon afterwards, Luigi Pirandello made a speech in Catania to mark Verga's eightieth birthday (1920); in it, with great ethical energy, he celebrated the most "anti-literary" of contemporary writers, capable of delving, "with a taciturn heart", down to the very depths of the small space that destiny had given him – a "writer of things" to oppose to the vacuous "writer of words" that was D'Annunzio. Giuseppe Antonio Borgese, in *Tempo di edificare* (Time to build), 1923, in the years of the cult of fragmentation, was to call for a new season of reconstruction on the ashes of artistic prose, and for a return to the majestic and symphonic novel that could build up a world and had precisely in Verga its first very robust architrave. A long and uninterrupted reflection, concentrating on the blind and painful, anti-rhetorical and anti-heroical, side of life during the 1930s made Verga the champion of a "complex simplicity", in the epoch of a very modern classicism capable of interpreting the "simple and natural voice of the great tradition", as Dino Giarrone puts it in his *Giovanni Verga*, published posthumously in 1941.

This classical and architectonic Verga, captured on the threshold of an epic, but of an epic having as its protagonists a mute and violated people, cut off from the magnificent and progressive destinies of national history, is the one we find in Guttuso's *Flight from Etna*. Vincenzo Consolo is right: *Flight from Etna* is a "vast poem in which man is for the first

Guttuso,
The Banquet, 1972.
Private collection.

time offended by nature". And this offence is no longer suffered and accepted as a natural calamity. Indeed, one can say that this crowd of humiliated people, "like an obstinate and proud avalanche of life" (quoting Consolo once again) has decided to abandon forever its inexorable destiny of silence. Guttuso, as Sciascia wrote, adopted a perspective which makes "things explode on the canvas or sheet", a perspective of "poverty", but, it must be added, no longer perceiving that poverty as an ontological horizon. Carefully observing the joyful scene of red and azure in *Fuga* (Flight), one realizes that its centre of gravity is actually outside the picture – where the tremendous story of nature ends that of history begins, a history which is to be one of deliverance and dignity, and no longer one of renunciation and grief.

It almost seems that Guttuso succeeds in breaking the stone circle of *I Malavoglia*. In so doing, he forces into it, at the very limits of a class solidarity which is still instinctive, Leopardi's appeal to the "social chain" of all men against a nature which is a mother to the human race but a stepmother by inclination. In sum, what we have in Guttuso is progressive Vergaism. Remarkably exact, in this sense, is another observation by Sciascia: "Guttuso's Italy is the Italy of De Sanctis", the De Sanctis, we will add, that gave us a Leopardi who was anything but Schopenhauerian, and wanted to arouse the interest of his fellow – countrymen in the new and positive literature coming from France. This, then, is the point: at the end of the 1930s, the painter from Bagheria, and not a novelist or other writer, was to prove the most authentic heir of Verga's example, which imposed itself on the best Italian culture, and an authentic heir because he was capable of assimilating and modifying that example, making it once again topical.

In order better to understand the meaning of this progressive reinterpretation of Verga, it is sufficient to compare Guttuso's *Flight* with a later work: the film *La terra trema* (1948) by Luchino Visconti, inspired, as is well known, by *I Malavoglia*. Audiences were to realize at once that Visconti did not escape from the tragedy, immobile and inconsolable, which is petrified in Verga's novel. At some points his Vergaism even appears didactic, quite apart from the lapse into dialect – a dialect difficult to understand even for Sicilians – and a peril that Verga superbly avoided. For this reason, Sciascia judged the film a "less modern work than *I Malavoglia*", despite the fact the "accidents" of history were more "modern and topical". One could say that, moving towards "constructed" painting, the imposing and majestic picture on which a true painter stakes his honour, as the artist himself often repeated, it is as if Guttuso had opened the door to a sort of historical novel, in works, so to speak, endowed with that extraordinary dynamic quality which always postulates a narrative "before" and "after", without the story "narrated" ever being entirely concluded within the picture itself. And this always occurring within a particular idea of the history of Italy. These are works with which everyone is familiar: *Zolfatari* (*Sulphur mine workers*), 1948; *Studio per "La Mafia" (Uccisione del capolega)* (*Study for "The Mafia": killing of the league leader*), 1948; *La battaglia di Ponte dell'Ammiraglio* (*The Battle of Ponte dell'Ammiraglio*), 1952-2; *La zolfara* (*The sulphur mine*), 1953; *L'occupazione delle terre* (*The occupation of the land*), 1957; *Io lo vi!* (*I saw*), 1966; *La notte di Gibellina* (*The night at Gibellina*), 1970; *I funerali di Togliatti* (*Togliatti's funeral*), 1972, just to mention a few.

It is equally true that the discovery of the historical novel, the biography of the nation inscribed in it, was also to be found in pictures with contemporary settings like *Boogie Woogie*, 1953-4. That biography was not to be restricted to an ideology which is that of actual historical, anti-providential novels, like *I vicere* by Federico De Roberto and *I vecchi e i giovani* by Luigi Pirandello. For Guttuso, history is not a road paved with ideological fossils, nor is it the ever-changing screen on which there is projected an unchanging story of minor transformations. It is not by chance that I previously mentioned Vincenzo Consolo: only he was to write a historical novel, *Il sorriso dell'ignoto marinaio*, comparable, in its feeling for the world, to Guttuso's large canvasses. In both, there is the identical Vittorini-style conviction that "not every man is a man, and not all humankind is human", but only those who are on the side of the suffering and the persecuted. In Guttuso, as in Consolo, there is always the perception, within social and political history, of a sacred history which is that of human suffering: the remarkable *Crucifixion*, 1941, is the clearest confirmation of this. This is a way of saying that the Communist faith, which in the man Guttuso was very strong, found in the painter a limit which was not only of a formal kind. It began with his instinctive cubist and anti-naturalist decomposition of reality, but extended to ideology: that metaphysics of suffering which derives from a Vergaism referring this time to nature and daily life, which Guttuso was born with in Bagheria. A metaphysics of suffering which – together, as is obvious, with its stylistic outrages – kept him safe, for good, from all lofty and false dictates of "Social realism", leading him instead towards a realism which was "conceptual", as Cesare Brandi puts it, wholly inside things, not in the least conditioned by any notion of art as mirroring. Of course, in some cases, as Sciascia wrote, his was "epic without poetry", but it never exhibited that "rhetorical and aestheticizing vitalism" which Carlo Levi cited. For example, in *The Battle of Ponte*

Guttuso,
Portrait of Montale 1939.
Galleria Nazionale d'Arte Moderna,
Rome.

*dell'Ammiraglio*, a picture which gives one an ideological image of Garibaldi no less enthusiastic than that of one of the Redshirts such as Giuseppe Cesare Abba, one need only concentrate on the oranges rolling out of the overturned basket to find once again the Guttuso free of rhetoric.

Clarification is also required regarding the celebratory rhetoric of certain paintings. Guttuso was often eloquent, but never edifying. And this eloquence, from an exclusively stylistic viewpoint, is to be regarded as one of his main merits. It is an eloquence which is also to be added to the other reasons which may account for that appreciation on the part of men of letters that is under examination. Guttuso made use of those oratorical elements that Borgese and Russo, from different positions, had brought back to literary culture after their excommunication by Croce, which had relegated them to the status of non-poetry. The poetry in Guttuso's pictures is, in the Russo and Borgese sense, a poetry which draws, while instensifying, on the plane of oratory. In this sense, in the field of painting, Guttuso achieves what Italian poets and prose writers could and would not. How could they, in a country in which vernacular poetry had been subjected to the verbal exhibitionism of Carducci and, worse, of D'Annunzio? Not to mention the fact that Eugenio Montale had by then forced men of letters to write about "what we are not", "what we do not want", thereby nurturing the great and very painful poetry of absence written in the 1930s.

Instead Guttuso, thanks to the mediation of Picasso, was to express in his pictures – from a point of view which we could define as metrical – those songs, those odes, those hymns, which Italian poetry was to be denied, at least until Pasolini

Guttuso,
Portrait of Moravia, 1940.
Museo di Brera, Milan.

wrote *Le Ceneri di Gramsci.* Isn't *The Battle of Ponte dell'Ammiraglio* a sort of song to Italy? Isn't *Togliatti's funeral* an ode? And as regards hymns it would be too easy to name the *Crucifixion.* In sum, Guttuso, to paraphrase a judgement by Moravia on the poet Pasolini, was the independent left-wing painter that Italy never had.

One last question: in the light of what has been said, should we perhaps conclude that the Guttuso closest to Italian literature is the one who, by and large, stops at *Togliatti's funeral*? Certainly not. From the 1970s, Guttuso's development continued to present extraordinary analogies with contemporary literature. Let us take the case of a writer who was, in all senses, very close to him: Leonardo Sciascia. The latter, starting from *Le Parrocchie di Regalpetra,* 1956, had pursued critical and progressive realism, but in the 1970s, starting from *Contesto,* 1971, as he grew more and more pessimistic about Italian affairs, he began to cultivate an idea of literature as an absolutely autonomous, orderly and rational cosmos, in opposition to the disorder of life. It could offer a system of eternal archetypes which would no longer be derived from reality, but were almost prefigurations of reality, the text being more and more entrusted to the intertextual network of quotations: an idea of literature which replaced Voltaire and Brancati with Borges and Pirandello. It appears to us that Guttuso's development was no different: one should think of pictures like *Il convivio* (*The banquet*), 1973; *Persistenza della metafisica* (*The persistence of metaphysics*), 1973; *Il Caffè Greco,* 1976 (the two different versions of which clearly document the meta-pictorial intensions, so to speak, the desire to rewrite art) or again, *Van Gogh porta il suo orecchio al bordello di Arles* (*Van Gogh takes his ear to the brothel in Arles*), 1978; *Le Allegorie* (*The allegories*), 1979; *Melancholia nova* (*New melancholy*), 1980; or *Spes contro Spem* (*Hope against hope*), 1982.

These are all works in which Guttuso seems to have arrived at an idea of painting as a circular and astral story, in which the icons of tradition are eternally repeated, reactivating themselves in a new context of meaning, always of a second degree, and as if translating into painting that feeling that Borges had for literature. Let us take the splendid *Banquet*: here, around a table in a little restaurant (perhaps in the Trastevere area of Rome) next to Picasso, over whose death Guttuso grieves, there is Apollinaire eating spaghetti while Gertrude Stein is busy with a fish, sitting together with the Harlequin-Pierrot and the Weeping Lady, those poignant Picasso creations. The picture becomes the absolutely autonomous world in which reality is reconstructed in accordance with a new grammar, that world in which the lie can prove truer than truth itself.

It would be inappropriate to conclude these considerations on Guttuso and Italian literature without once again mentioning the speech that Luigi Pirandello made in Catania in 1920. In this speech we have a first rough draft of that sentiment that Sciascia was to encompass in the concept of "Sicilianness": "The Sicilians, almost all of them, have an instinctive fear of life, so that they withdraw into themselves, aloof, satisfied with little, provided it gives them security. They diffidently perceive the contrast between their closed souls and the open nature around them, bright with sunlight. They retreat into themselves even more, because they do not trust this open space, isolated on all sides by the sea, that is to say, cut off and alone. Each person makes and becomes an island himself, and enjoys by himself

– but barely, if he has it – his little joy: alone, taciturn, without seeking comfort, he suffers his grief, often desperate. But there are those who escape; those who not only materially cross the sea, but, braving that instinctive fear, take themselves away (or think they take themselves away) from those few profound qualities that make them islands in themselves and, led by a certain fantastic sensuality, they seek wider horizon while depriving themselves of all passion, or rather smothering and betraying their true, hidden passion, with an ephemeral ambition for life. Verga, as a young man, was one of these". Guttuso when young was also one of these Sicilians ambitious for life. And we do not believe he deluded himself, even for an instant, that he was taking himself away from "those few profound qualities" that, according to Pirandello, makes all Sicilians "island in themselves". Many, starting from Sciascia, have written that whatever he chose to paint, he always painted Sicily. It would not be difficult to demonstrate this. Just as it would not be difficult to outline, through his paintings, the diagram of his "Sicilianness", within the impatience and aggressiveness of the colours, as well as the fire of passions. Let us take a masterpiece like *La Vucciria*: we shall never again get out of our minds the image of that woman seen from the back, her body indulging in soft Mediterranean laziness, at the exact centre of an obscene labyrinth of smells and flavours. Guttuso is one of very few painters who succeed in painting with fresh appetite, who are able to return beyond food, beyond sex, to the primeval origin of life. But such an appetite, as Goffredo Parise pointed out, has the inexorable counterpoint of a continual *memento mori*. Light and mourning, then: but this would be another subject, and one no less complicated.

Guttuso,
Hope against hope, 1982.
Private collection.

# WORKS

Ritratto del padre Gioacchino (Portrait of his father Gioacchino), 1930

La donna del marinaio (The sailor's woman), 1932

Naufraghi (The shipwrecked), 1932

Palinuro (Palinurus), 1932

Bambini in festa (Children playing), 1935

Fantasia (Fantasy), 1936–37

Amanti (Lovers), 1932

Animali nella notte (Animals in the night), 1935

Il figliol prodigo (The prodigal son),1935

Autoritratto con sciarpa e ombrello (Self-portrait with scarf and umbrella), 1936

Cristo deriso (The Mocking of Christ), 1938

Fucilazione in campagna (Execution in the country), 1938

Cranio d'ariete (Ram's skull), 1938

Studio per la Fuga dall'Etna (Study for Flight from Etna), 1938

Studio per la Fuga dall'Etna (Study for Flight from Etna), 1938–39

Fuga dall'Etna (Flight from Etna), 1938–39

Gente nello studio (People in the studio), 1938

Interno con gabbia (Interior with cage), 1939

Famiglia (Family), 1940

Ritratto di Mimise con il cappello rosso (Portrait of Mimise with red hat), 1940

Natura morta (Still life),1940

Natura morta (Still life), 1940–41

Fiasco candela e bollitore (Bottle, candle and kettle), 1940–41

Natura morta sul tavolo rosso (Still life on red table), 1942

Cesta e bottiglie (Basket and bottles), 1941–42

Un angolo dello studio a Via Pompeo Magno (A corner of the studio in Via Pompeo Magno), 1941–42

Crocifissione (Crucifixion), 1940–41

Crocifissione in una stanza (Crucifixion in a room), 1940

Battaglia e cavalli feriti (Battle scene with wounded horses), 1942–43

Massacro (Massacre), 1943

Trionfo della morte (Triumph of death), 1943

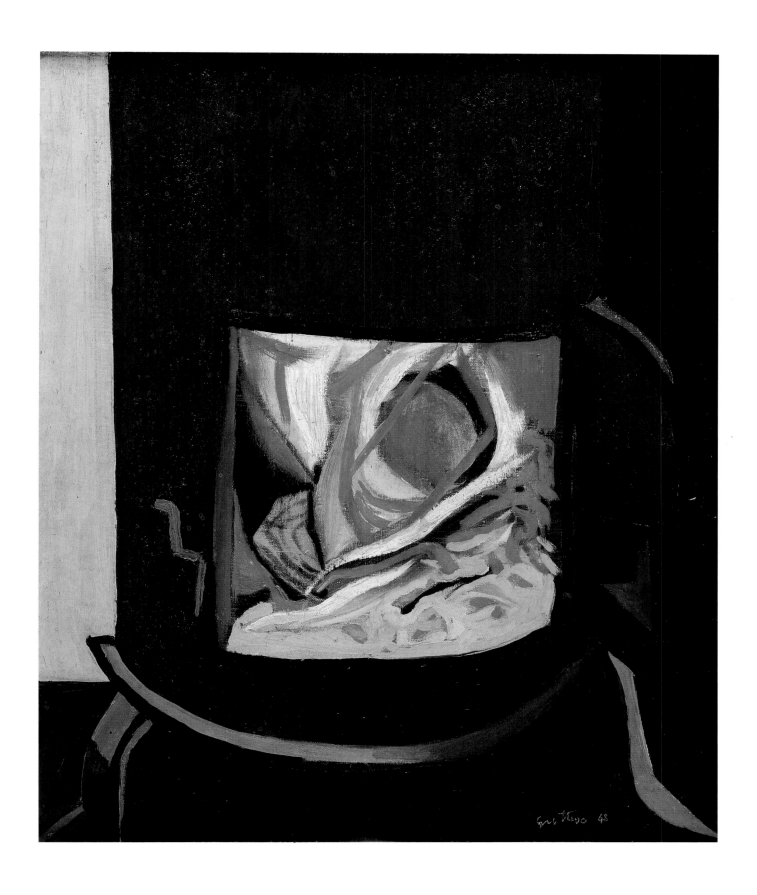

Stufa a legna (Wood burner), 1948

Studio per la spiaggia (Study for "The beach"), 1955

Quattro figure sulla spiaggia (Four figures on the beach), 1957

Tre fumatori (Three smokers), 1958

Fumatore (The smoker), 1958

Fumatore (The smoker), 1958

La discussione (The discussion), 1959–60

Ricci (Sea urchins), 1950

Fichi d'india (Prickly pears), 1959

Tetti a Velate d'inverno (Roofs at Velate in winter), 1957

Alberi a Velate (Trees at Velate), 1958

Bosco di Velate (Velate wood), 1958

Nudo (Nude), 1961

Natura morta con martello e forchetta (Still life with hammer and fork), 1958

Angolo di studio (Corner of the studio), 1961

Fichi d'india (Prickly pears), 1962

Cactus, 1962

Natura morta (Still life), 1963

Tetti su Via Leonina (Roofs on Via Leonina), 1962

Carretto con cavoli (Cart with cabbages), 1973

La Vucciria (The Vucciria), 1974

Teschio e cravatte (Skulls and ties), 1979

Telefoni (Telephones), 1980

Sfascio di automobili (The breaker's yard), 1979

Nudo di donna (Nude), 1980

Prato di Velate con ortensie (Meadow at Velate with hortensias), 1984

Sera a Velate (Evening at Velate), 1980

**Woman with white stocking (after Courbet), 1935.** Sepia,  25 x 29,5 cm
Private collection

**Reclining female figure reading, 1936.** Pencil, 27,5 x 37,5 cm
Private collection

**Massacre, 1939.** Watercolour on paper mounted on canvas, 22 x 28 cm
Private collection

**Study from Picasso's Crucifixion, 1938.** India ink, 31 x 44 cm
Private collection

**Nude after Bernini, 1939.** Pencil, 37,6 x 24,5 cm
Galleria d'Arte Moderna e Contemporanea "Renato Guttuso" di Villa Cattolica, Bagheria

Reclining woman, 1939. India ink, 30,5 x 23,6 cm
Galleria d'Arte Moderna e Contemporanea "Renato Guttuso" di Villa Cattolica, Bagheria

**Dog, 1935.** Pencil, 18,3 x 24,5 cm
Galleria d'Arte Moderna e Contemporanea "Renato Guttuso" di Villa Cattolica, Bagheria

Two figures (David and Goliath), 1939. India ink, 33,4 x 28,3 cm
Galleria d'Arte Moderna e Contemporanea "Renato Guttuso" di Villa Cattolica, Bagheria

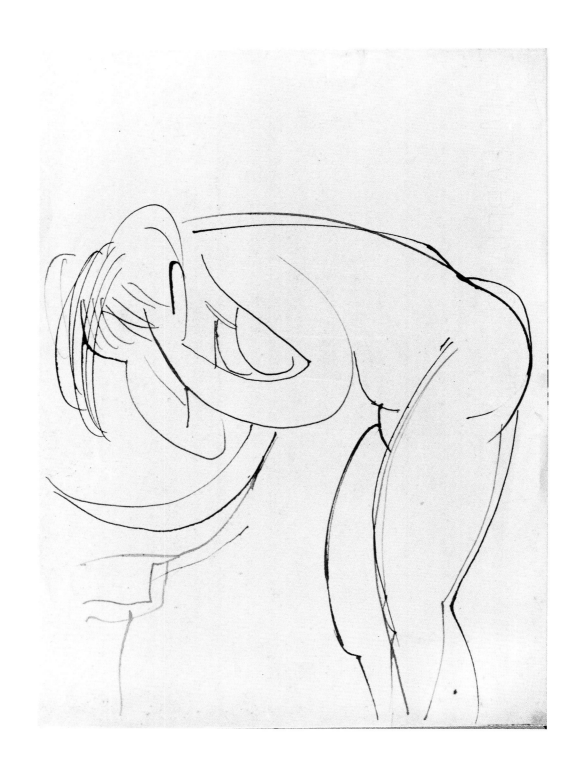

**Nude woman bending, 1939.** India ink, 36 x 26,5 cm
Galleria d'Arte Moderna e Contemporanea "Renato Guttuso" di Villa Cattolica, Bagheria

**Study for Mary Magdalene, 1940–41**. Ink, pencil and watercolour, 32,5 x 18,5 cm
Private collection

**Shootings, 1942.** Ink, 25 x 35 cm
Private collection

Triumph of Death, 1940. India ink, 33 x 39,5 cm
Private collection

The insurrection, 1945. Ink, 27 x 20 cm
Private collection

**Female figure, 1961.** India ink and watercolour, 30,5 x 22,7 cm
Private collection

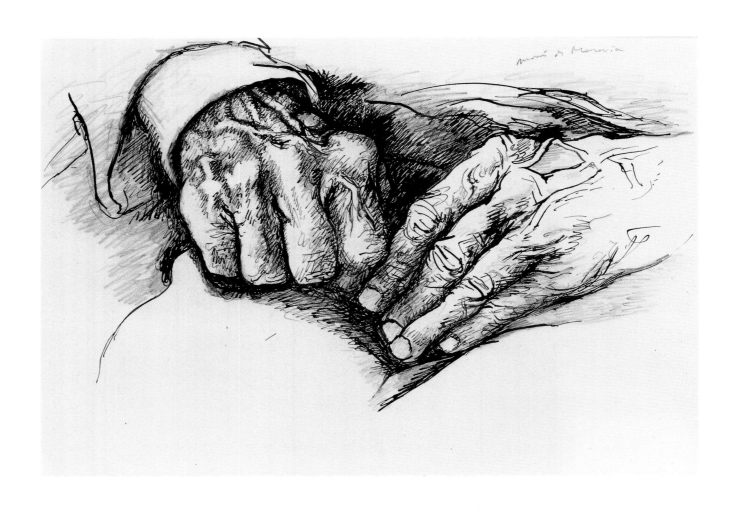

Moravia's hands, 1982. Pencil and India ink, 35 x 50 cm
Private collection

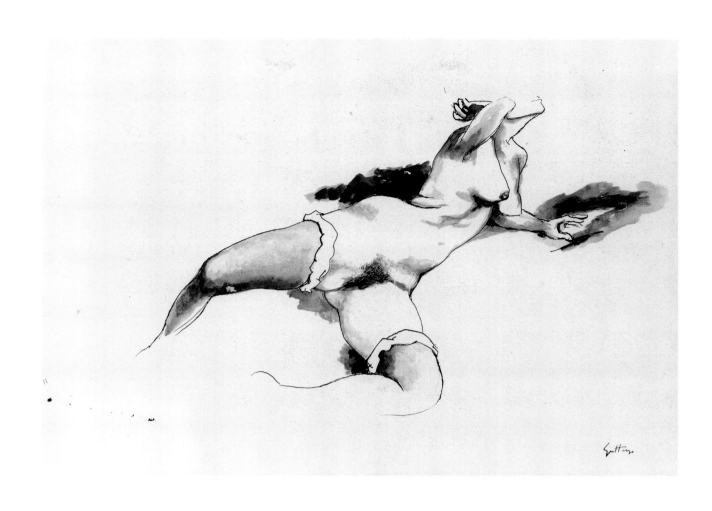

**Female figure, 1985.** India ink, watercolour and acrylic, 50 x 75 cm
Private collection

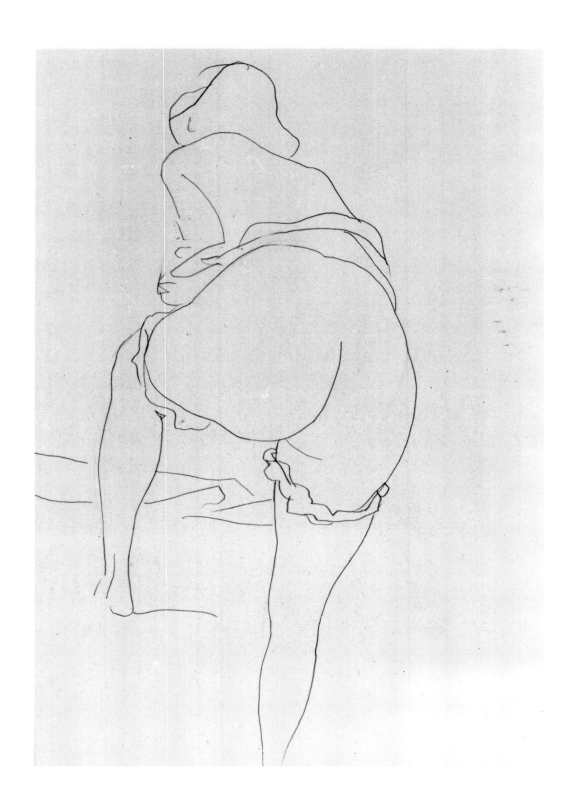

Study of nude, 1982. Pencil, 50 x 33 cm
Private collection

**Nude of woman kneeling on bed, 1984.** India ink, watercolour and acrylic, 57,2 x 38,3 cm
Private collection

**Study for Incommunicability, 1979.** Pencil on cardboard, 35,5 x 32,5 cm
Private collection

# WORKS

*edited by* Fabio **Carapezza Guttuso**

Each work is listed with its medium, dimensions, inscriptions and present location. The Catalogue raisonné numbers refer to the *Catalogo ragionato generale dei dipinti di Renato Guttuso*, edited by Enrico Crispolti, vols. I-IV, Milan, Giorgio Mondadori, 1983-1990, hereafter referred to as Catalogue raisonné; the reader is referred to the latter for bibliography and the list of exhibitions in which the work was exhibited. Exhibitions subsequent to the publication of the Catalogue are listed here, using the following abbreviations:

Tübingen, 1991: *Guttuso*, Kunsthalle Tübingen, Kunstmuseum Düsseldorf, Kunstverein Hamburg, 1991-92. Catalogue: Verlag Gerd Hatje, Stuttgart.
Italian Art 20th Cent., 1989: *Italian Art in the 20th Century*, Royal Academy of Arts, London, 1989. Catalogue: Prestel Verlag, Münich.

Arte italiana, 1989: *Arte italiana presenze 1900-1945*, Palazzo Grassi, Venezia, 1989. Catalogue: Bompiani, Milano.
Turin, 1992: Guttuso, Galleria d'Arte Nuova Gissi , Turin, November 1992-January 1993.
Pittura e realtà, 1993; *Pittura e realtà*, Palazzo dei Diamanti, Ferrara 1993. Catalogue: Edizione Tosi, Ferrara.
Bergamo, 1993: *Gli anni del premio Bergamo*, Galleria d'Arte Moderna e Contemporanea e Accademia Carrara, Bergamo, September 1993 - January 1994. Catalogue: Electa, Milano.
Arte della Libertà, 1995: *Arte della Libertà*, Palazzo Ducale, Genoa, November 1995 - March1996. Catalogue: Mazzotta, Milan.
Finale Ligure, 1995: *Renato Guttuso*, Finale Ligure, October 1995-January 1996.

**Portrait of his father Gioacchino, 1930**
Oil on canvas, 65 x 55 cm
Signed top left: "Renato Guttuso ex patris suis praeclara efigie summa cum diligentia hanc parvam tabulam extraxit"
Galleria d'Arte Moderna e Contemporanea 'Renato Guttuso' di Villa Cattolica, Bagheria

Catalogue raisonné,
vols. I and IV: no. 30/3
Tübingen, 1991

"I was born when my father was already at a ripe age, almost fifty, and I was the only son. Because of this age difference, there existed between us the kind of affectionate relations that you have between grandfather and grandson, without the clashes between father and son due to the generation gap: basically, we had skipped one generation, and hence there was great tenderness." Unpublished letter (Archivi Guttuso)

**The sailor's woman, 1932**
Oil on canvas, 80 x 65 cm
Signed, dated and dedicated bottom left "a Peppino Fecarotta amico dei poeti con affetto, Renato"
(to Peppino Fecarotta friend of poets with affection, Renato)
Private Collection

Catalogue raisonné,
vols. I and IV: no. 32/2
Tübingen, 1991

"I had such a great desire to see it, this sea of mine that I have not yet tired of observing. Now it's in front of me, I see it beyond the window of my studio, bright and blue, it is very beautiful." (Letter from Renato Guttuso to Brajo and Bettina Fuso, 1932. Archivi Guttuso, Rome)

**The shipwrecked, 1932**
Oil on canvas, 130 x 100 cm
Signed and dated on right, halfway up
Private Collection

Catalogue raisonné,
vols. I and IV: no. 32/4

"The mythological reference is to the Mediterranean Sea, from the unforgettable Magna Graecia to the sea of its fishermen, of Sicilian sailors."
(Enrico Crispolti, *Leggere Guttuso*, Mondadori, Milan 1987)

**Palinurus, 1932**
Oil on canvas, 100 x 136 cm
Signed and dated bottom right
Private Collection

Catalogue raisonné,
vols. I and IV: no. 32/5.

"Nudus in ignota Palinure iacebis arena" - Virgil's verse echoes in the mind of the artist who had found the naked body of a fisherman thrown up by the storm on the beach of not unknown Aspra [a fishing village near Bagheria], still clinging to the wreck of his boat." (Franco Grasso, in the catalogue to the exhibition of works by Renato Guttuso at the Palazzo dei Normanni, Palermo. Publ. by Sicilian Regional Parliament, 1971)

"The brush stroke is free, fluid, fiery, imbued in pure colour; bodies, drapery, the objects themselves, move, bend, tremble, driven by an inner restlessness, by a vital impulse, by a rebellious energy " (Franco Grasso, op. cit.)

**Lovers, 1932**
Gouache on paper glued on cardboard,
38 x 51 cm
Signed and dated bottom centre
Galleria d'Arte Moderna e
Contemporanea 'Renato Guttuso'
di Villa Cattolica, Bagheria

Catalogue raisonné,
vol. IV: no. 32/7.

"Constructed, like the layout of a chromatic scene, always in broad sections, between the red cloth heaped up at the bottom (one would say the fascia is half made up of volcanic rocks) and the black sky in the background, the flesh of the free little bodies cutting loose from it, and the creased white of the clothes of the children in the foreground, with a bright chiaroscuro effect, it is an almost oneiric painting." (Enrico Crispolti, op. cit.)

**Children playing, 1935**
Oil on hardboard, 96 x 83 cm
Signed and dated bottom left
Private Collection

Catalogue raisonné,
vols. I and IV: no. 35/2

"For Guttuso art is first of all a moral solution. His idea is to find a way in which ideas and things come together to form a single creation. An expressive state circulates in every part of the picture. Objects and bodies in Renato Guttuso's painting give a sensation of limp straws shaken by the wind. High horizons and long intersecting arches predominate, dilations and contractions like those of a breathing body". (Renato Birolli, Il ventuno, Milan, 1935)

**The prodigal son, 1935**
Oil on canvas, 60 x 42 cm
"Donazione Boschi di Stefano", Civiche
Raccolte d'Arte, Milan

Catalogue raisonné,
vols. I and IV: no. 35/8

**Animals in the night, 1935**
Oil on hardboard, 44 x 60 cm
Signed bottom right
On the verso title and dedication
"animals passing in the night to Lino,
affectionately 1935"
Private Collection

Catalogue raisonné,
vols. I and IV: no. 35/17

"Moravia: Is it difficult for you to do a self-portrait?
Guttuso: A portrait always creates problems. But they are always stimulating problems. I would like to do a large picture entirely made up of portraits. A sort of study, with lots of friends." (Interview with Guttuso by Moravia, 1982)

"Those who know Guttuso well, are familiar with his character, know what it means for him to paint a portrait because they know what it means for him to be a realist. That is to say, they know that it is equivalent to living the relationship with things and the relationship with himself." (Giuliano Briganti, "Ritratti ed autoritratti", introduction to the catalogue of the exhibition at the Galleria dell'Oca, Rome, 1983)

**Self-portrait with scarf
and umbrella, 1936**
Oil on hardboard, 71 x 55 cm
Signed and dated bottom right
Private Collection

Catalogue raisonné,
vols. I and IV: no. 36/1
Tübingen, 1991

**Fantasy, 1936-7**
Oil on hardboard, 71 x 54 cm
Galleria d'Arte Moderna e
Contemporanea 'Renato Guttuso'
di Villa Cattolica, Bagheria

Catalogue raisonné,
vols. I and IV: no. 36-37/4

"In this young painter there is (...) a lyrical need, which seeks a way in which to express itself... the anxious desire to shake traditional forms, to bring in through those cracks the reflections of a new sensibility, and the designs of a new ambition..."
(Nino Savarese, introduction to the catalogue of the exhibition at the Cometa Gallery, Rome, 1938)

**Execution in the country, 1938**
Oil on canvas, 108 x 84.5 cm
Signed and dated bottom right
On the verso "Renato Guttuso 1939"
(date of first exhibition)
Galleria Nazionale d'Arte Moderna, Rome

Catalogue raisonné,
vols. I and IV: no. 38/2
Italian Art 20th Cent., 1989
Tübingen, 1991

"In Milan I met Vittorini. He travelled around with a suitcase full of manifestoes and clandestine printed matter, he travelled all over Italy and was writing *Conversazione in Sicilia*. It was in the wake of that revolutionary book, and echoing its title, that I painted my Execution in the country, dedicated to the death of Garcia Lorca, killed in that period by the Spanish fascists." (Interview with Guttuso by Mario Farinella, 1971)

"The white of the shirt is like a shout in the darkness of the scene"
(Cesare Brandi, Guttuso, Fabbri, Milano 1983)

**People in the studio, 1938**
Oil on board, 63 x 88 cm
Signed and dated bottom right
Galleria dell'Oca, Rome

Catalogue raisonné,
vols. I and IV: no. 38/3
Pittura e realtà, 1993

The painting shows Mimise Guttuso (the painter's wife), Aldo Natili, Armando Pizzinato, Mario Mafai and Antonietta Raphael.
"At that time he lived in Piazza Melozzo da Forlì, a modern building like a barracks, with a big terrace and a big room with big windows which served as his studio, in which he also slept. Then there was a corridor and two other rooms which were empty because he was penniless, but he needed them for when young artists came to Rome who were in the same condition and he put them up..." (Kris Mancuso in *L'Ora*, Palermo, 1971)

**The mocking of Christ , 1938**
Oil on hardboard, 46 x 30.5 cm
Signed bottom right
On the verso "1938 Questo dipinto
è autentico. In fede, Renato Guttuso"
(1938 This painting is authentic.
In faith, Renato Guttuso)
Camera dei Deputati, Rome

Catalogue raisonné,
vols. I and IV: no. 38/46

**Ram's skull, 1938**
Oil on paper mounted on canvas,
29 x 41.8 cm
Archivi Guttuso, Rome

Catalogue raisonné,
vols. I and IV: no. 38/57

"Now for the first time there appears the grinning ram's head, which for Guttuso at that time represented the memory of the Spanish Civil War. Not as a symbol but as a strongly evocative object, which in being rendered ghostly and skeletal harked back to the horror and fear in the apparently ghostly coexistence of things and evoked an experience of life consumed down to the dregs." (Werner Haftmann, "Renato Guttuso: man and work", in the catalogue to Guttuso, Kunsthalle Tubingen, Kunstmuseum Dusseldorf, Kunstverein Hamburg, 1991-2, Verlag Gerd Hatje, Stuttgart)

**Study for Flight from Etna, 1938**
Oil on paper mounted on canvas,
132 x 100 cm
Signed and dated bottom right
Private Collection

Catalogue raisonné,
vols. I and IV: no. 38/48

**Study for Flight from Etna, 1938–39**
Oil on hardboard, 81 x 66 cm
Signed bottom right
On the verso "Guttuso bozzetto per una
pittura" (Guttuso sketch for a painting)
Private Collection, Rome

Catalogue raisonné,
vols. I and IV: no. 38-39/13 and 13a

"The anxiety of painting in those years was, I remember very well, contained
emotionally and visually in that work, where from that very time I was struck,
and disturbed, by the dialectic, at that time difficult for me to understand, between
forces and figures that seemed to precipitate towards the centre of the picture, that
rough and derelict chair, and at the same time to run away from it, splinters of bone
and mangled bones." (Giovanni Testori, in the catalogue to *Renato Guttuso: Mostra
antologica dal 1931 ad oggi*, Palazzo della Pilotta, Parma, 1963)

"[The painting] presents itself as anguish, the rejection of fascist atrocity symbolised
by the insensate fury of the elements, with the red of the lava like live magma."
(Cesare Brandi, *Guttuso*, Fabbri, Milan, 1983)

**Flight from Etna, 1938–39**
Oil on canvas, 144 x 254 cm
Signed and dated bottom right
Galleria Nazionale d'Arte Moderna, Rome

Catalogue raisonné,
vols. I and IV: no. 38-39/14
Italian Art 20th cent., 1989
Arte italiana, 1989
Tübingen, 1991
Pittura e realtà, 1993
Bergamo, 1993
Art and Power, 1995

"In 1939/40 Guttuso started his experiments again with a series of magnificent still
lifes. A rigid grid acts like a chain, enclosing the structure of space. This is Cubism
of a particular sort: Guttuso returns to the spatial dimension of the Cubist picture
but stops before the opening up and dissolving of the object, through which classical
Cubism objectively qualified the phenomenological and almost autonomous field
of the picture. Guttuso re-emphasised the autonomy of the single object
in its existential dignity: the Italian awareness of the original compactness of things
prevented him from breaking down the realistic image." (Werner Haftmann, op. cit.)

**Interior with cage, 1939**
Oil on board, 70 x 50 cm
Signed and dated bottom right
Private Collection

Catalogue raisonné,
vol. I: no. 39/20
Pittura e realtà, 1993

**Still life, 1940**
Oil on board, 55 x 75 cm
Signed and dated bottom centre
Galleria d'Arte Nuova Gissi, Turin

Catalogue raisonné,
vol. I: no. 40/2 bis

**Family, 1940**
Oil on canvas, 65 x 50 cm
Signed bottom left
On the verso "Guttuso Famiglia"
Private Collection,

Catalogue raisonné,
vol. I: no. 40/3

**Portrait of Mimise
with red hat, 1940**
Oil on canvas, 55 x 45.5 cm
Signed and dated bottom right
Private Collection

Catalogue raisonné,
vols. I and IV: no. 40/33
Tübingen, 1991

"My dearest Ginevra and Marcello,
You can understand me, Mimise was not only my companion. She was a fact in my life,
part of my flesh, of my kind: if I were not afraid of being rhetorical I would say with
conviction that she was part of my 'culture'.
Of that knowledge which unites two people as flesh and maybe something more."
(Letter of 10/10/1986 to his friends Marcello and Ginevra Carapezza, five days
after the death of his wife Mimise. Archivi Guttuso, Rome)

**Crucifixion in a room, 1940**
Oil on canvas, 64.5 x 47.5 cm
On the verso "Guttuso 940"
Private Collection Mario Grimaldi,
Salerno

Catalogue raisonné,
vols. I: no. 38/39 and IV: no. 40/42

"I believe that around 1940 we were not better than the young people 'of today',
nor worse. There is no need to write history with 'ifs' in order to state that if the best
young people had been twenty around 1940, they would have done, more or less,
in that situation, what we did. Birolli, Morlotti, Cassinari and Treccani and the others,
including me, were not the only young people in Italy. There were others, some very
gifted, who did not participate in any way in that moral revolt that *Corrente*
essentially was... No judgement on *Corrente* can avoid taking its cultural and historical
limitations into account. In the years around 1941 the significance of *Corrente* was
clarified and its various positions were defined. By that time expressionism had become
a reference point for everyone, although some of us rather perceived its decadent
aspect, others the civil lesson." (Renato Guttuso, "Dialogo sulla pittura" (1962),
in *Mestiere di pittore*, De Donato, Bari, 1972)

**Still life, 1940-41**
Oil on board, 55 x 40 cm
Signed and dated halfway up on right
Private Collection Antonio Stellatelli,
Monza

Catalogue raisonné,
vols. I and IV: no. 40-41/10
Tübingen, 1991
Pittura e realtà, 1993

"At that time I was, together with other young people of my generation, challenging
Morandi, because he also seemed to us the symbol of a general reductive situation,
connected more to the twilight of post-Impressionism than to the promptings and
undertakings of the European avant-garde.... That polemic, however, at least as far as I
was concerned, did not ignore a dialectic rapport, and in my still lifes of 40, 41 and 42
the links with Morandi are explicit, together with the contradictions through the
presence of some Morandi-style objects... and even the spiral-shaped opaline bottle."
(Guttuso, in the catalogue of the exhibition *Omaggio a Morandi* at the Galleria
Il Milione, Milan, 1966)

**Kettle, candle and bottle, 1940-1**
Oil on board, 53.5 x 73 cm
Signed top right
On the verso signed and dated: "Guttuso 40"
Galleria dello Scudo, Verona

Catalogue raisonné,
vols. I and IV: no. 40-41/3
Tübingen, 1991
Pittura e realtà, 1993
Turin, 1992

"Objects on the table, 1940... which Guttuso defines the first of the group
of 'still lifes' painted in the studio in Via Pompeo Magno from 1940 to 1942, in which
however I glimpse a rougher type of modelling which makes me think of later ones.
(One should see the basket, bottle and candlestick)."
(Raffaele De Grada, "I Guttuso della collezione de Ponti", Catalogue of the exhibition
*Guttuso*, San Gimignano, 1970)

"Started at the end of 1940, with numerous preparatory drawings and sketches and realized in two separate stages in 1941, the big painting polarises a theme which already obsessed Guttuso's imagination in those years. It was an engaged response to the violent times in which he was living. Between the first version and the final one there is the progressive passage from the usual expressionism, with a realistic and naturalistic grounding, to formal and chromatic syncopation which more openly signified the will to use a stylistic cipher, which came out of Guttuso's reflections on the Cubist tradition." (Enrico Crispolti, op. cit.)

On 17 September 1942 *L'Avvenire d'Italia* published a communique from the chancery of the bishop's curia in Bergamo: "By order of His Eminence the Bishop warning is given to all the clergy of the diocese and clergy passing through our city that they are forbidden to go to the exhibition of the Bergamo award on pain of suspension *a divinis ipso facto incurrenda*. Parish priests will also warn the faithful that it is not seemly to visit the exhibition."

**Crucifixion, 1940–1**
Oil on canvas, 200 x 200 cm
Signed bottom right
Galleria Nazionale d'Arte Moderna, Rome

Catalogue raisonné, vols. I and IV: no. 40-41/25
Tübingen, 1991
*The body on the cross*, Musée Picasso, Paris, November 1992-March 1993.
Bergamo, 1993
Italian Art 20th Cent., 1989
Arte italiana, 1989
*The Italian Metamorphosis 1943/68*, Guggenheim Museum, New York, October 1994-March 1995.

---

"After the Crucifixion there began a period of greater independence of the model, in which form is developed with the flexibility of timeless imagination. Cubist spatial fracture and expressionistic tendencies give way to a free play of colour oppositions, in which light, used imaginatively, splits it in two, cleaves it, lengthens it and arrests it: as in a process of fusion, the various pieces of wreckage are cemented together in a new and incontrovertible way. Some pictures from this very happy period are among the most alive creations of the century." (Cesare Brandi, *Guttuso*, Fabbri, Milan, 1983)

**Basket and bottles, 1941–2**
Oil on canvas, 50 x 61 cm
Signed top right
Raccolta di Arte Contemporanea
Alberto Della Ragione, Florence

Catalogue raisonné,
vols. I and IV: no. 41-42/1

---

"As if he wanted to widen the walls of the studio in Via Pompeo Magno, Guttuso opens the windows allowing the landscape to encompass the intimacy of the room. I consider this group of compositions (I would no longer define them 'still lifes') as to be implicitly against the scepticism of the formal 'still life' which does not go beyond the idealisation of the object.... They mark a turning point in Italian art in the period." (Raffaele De Grada, "I Guttuso della collezione de Ponti", Catalogue of the exhibition *Guttuso*, San Gimignano, 1970)

"When the artist enters his studio he cannot leave the dust on the threshold, as a Muslim entering the mosque takes off his shoes. He must take the dust in with him, for I am convinced that a painter, though painting things and not ideas, always ends up showing his ideas through the things painted."
(Interview with Renato Guttuso by Bruno Romani, *Secolo XIX*, Genova, 1-6-72)

**A corner of the studio in Via Pompeo Magno, 1941–2**
Oil on canvas, 80 x 65 cm
Signed top right
Civici Musei e Gallerie di Storia e Arte, Galleria d'Arte Moderna, Udine

Catalogue raisonné,
vols. I and IV: no. 41-42/3
Tübingen, 1991

---

"Struggle is being waged on the earth in the shape of wars, revolutions, massacres and exterminations. Man commits his life, wears it out, smashes it for the conquest of a dignity, or for well-being, perhaps simply for hope ... Man has lain under wrath, starting from the most ancient of his myths. Nor can the artist say that his kingdom is another, an abstract kingdom of colour, shapes, words, sounds, a kingdom like a refuge in which he can at least live without all these tortures. This kingdom is impossible, at least for a painter.... For a living work needs the man who is creative to be angry and to express his anger in the way most suited to him. A work of art is always the sum of the pleasures and griefs of the man who has created it. I do not mean that it is necessary for a painter to belong to one party or another, to make war, or to start a revolution, but it is necessary that he act in painting in the way that those who make war or start a revolution act. In short, like those who die for something."
(Renato Guttuso, "Pensieri sulla pittura", *Primato*, Rome, 15 August 1941)

**Battle scene with wounded horses, 1942–3**
Oil on canvas, 50 x 61 cm
Signed bottom right
On the verso "Renato Guttuso, proprietà della galleria della Spiga, Milano" (Renato Guttuso, property of Spiga Gallery, Milan)
Galleria Nazionale d'Arte Moderna, Rome

Catalogue raisonné,
vols. I and IV: no. 42-43/2
Arte della Libertà, 1995

---

"Meanings will become crystals: and your red, Guttuso, will seep back into history/ like a river which has disappeared in the desert./ Your red will be the red, the red of the worker/ and the red of the poet, a single red/ which will stand for the reality of a struggle,/ hope, victory and pity." (Pier Paolo Pasolini, "Il rosso di Guttuso")

**Still life on red table, 1942**
Oil on canvas, 60 x 80 cm
Signed bottom centre
On the verso signed and dated "Guttuso 42"
Private Collection Antonio Stellatelli, Monza

Catalogue raisonné,
vol. I: 42/13

**Massacre, 1943**
Oil on canvas, 55 x 70.5 cm
Raccolta di Arte Contemporanea Alberto
Della Ragione, Florence

Catalogue raisonné,
vols. I and IV: no. 43/1

"Every specific question, dear Ennio, turns on a single point: the quantity of living flesh that will be in a picture or book. Art is not made through divine grace or revelation. God has nothing to do with it, nor has grace, but only the quantity of ourselves as blood, intelligence, moral life that is hurled into it."
(Letter from Guttuso to Ennio Morlotti, 1943. Archivi Guttuso, Rome)

**Triumph of Death, 1943**
Oil on canvas, 55 x 55 cm
Galleria Nazionale d'Arte Moderna, Rome

Catalogue raisonné,
vols. I and IV: no. 43/2
Tübingen, 1991
Arte della Libertà, 1995

"In 1938 Brandi sent me a postcard with a reproduction of *Guernica*. I kept it in my wallet until 43, like the ideal membership card of a party. That modern *Triumph of Death* in which bestiality took the place of fatality opened up the way to a lot of thoughts. Guernica was a key (not a dictionary)." (Guttuso, "Dialogo sulla pittura" in *Mestiere di pittore*, op. cit.).
"Looking at a big panel by Picasso (*Guernica*) I think of *Triumph of Death* at Palazzo Sclafani in Palermo... One should compare these two 'battles'. In the Palermo encaustic the medieval sentiment of equality in the face of death, old age, youth, the poor and the powerful, in Picasso's picture a tragedy, and a modern terror, without resignation under the light of the electric lamps. The two works have very strong inner links, but also formal links. The skeletal horse of the triumph becomes in Picasso, mad (the head is almost the same). Death with a scythe in its belt becomes a measureless arm holding a lamp, the dog of the noble gentleman walking in the country becomes a bull (top left corner in both paintings), the group of praying people a strange tangle of dying and dead (bottom left corner). Along the base of the two panels from left to over halfway are the dead; bottom right a group of great people in ancient Catalonia, in Picasso a woman fleeing and one shouting. Top right, the fountain of youth becomes a house gutted by light. (Guttuso, "Appunti sulla pittura", 1940)

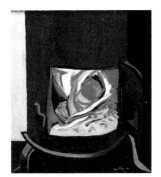

**Wood burner, 1948**
Oil on canvas, 70 x 60 cm
Signed and dated bottom right
Banca di Roma

Catalogue raisonné,
vols. I and IV: no. 48/21

**Sea urchins, 1950**
Oil on canvas, 30 x 40 cm
On the verso signed and dated
"Guttuso 20 Ag 1950"
Archivi Guttuso, Rome

Catalogue raisonné,
vols. I and IV: no. 50/40

The work belongs to the cycle of paintings done at Scilla in Calabria, where Guttuso spent the summers of 49 and 51, giving rise to the "Scilla school".

"It is necessary to insist on the 'naturalness' of Guttuso's art, on the moral energy that upholds and explains it. It would be useless to expect of Guttuso a topical formalism, which has no relevance to him, is not part of his nature: a useless and absurd expectation, which is mentioned only because some people, faced with the Terni and Scilla scenes, shout out about treason and accuse the painter of opportunism. This is unjust because Guttuso adheres to the elementary values of life, to every expression revealing primeval passion and sentiments, i.e. touching man's substance in the violence of instincts. Guttuso's participation is natural and spontaneous, and is fully present right from the start, that is to say from his expressionistic 'protests'."
(Giuseppe Marchiori, *Panorama dell'arte italiana*, 1968)

**Study for "The Beach", 1955**
Oil on canvas, 60 x 75 cm
Signed bottom right
Archivi Guttuso, Rome

Catalogue raisonné,
vols. II and IV: no. 55/46

"Guttuso believes in human dignity and its relevance to the meaning of art. (...) To this credo Guttuso has brought a flaming intensity of vision and a stark humility. (...) He himself has spoken of the need he feels to transcend purely esthetic considerations and "to hit something in the heart". He adds: " to do this, one must have the courage and the honor to go against the current, to be unpopolar and to paint, if necessary, even ugly pictures". Perhaps The Beach is such a picture. It is also memorable, and the many sketches Guttuso made for it are extraordinary in their ferocious conviction and, once or twice, in their tender restraint. Graciousness is not usually the quality to look for in Guttuso's art, but his total nervous involvement in the finest of his painting and drawings repays our closest attention" (J.T. Soby, in the catalogue of the exhibition at the Aca and Heller Galleries, New York 1958)

"That inner possibility of dialogue goes on even when, more recently, you abandoned the themes more openly "populist", themes for one that I would call "interclassista" (The Beach - one of the most ambitious paintings, and also one of the most bravely meditated modern paintings, after "La Grande Jatte" of Seurat). There in fact you nod slightly towards the early protocubist Signorelli of Orvieto or towards the ceiling of Michelangelo. In fact I remember what I was saying a few days ago about the painting of yours in which a girl is clinging to a motor-scooter driver: "A Sybil climbing up ... Via Sistina" (Roberto Longhi, in the catalogue of the exhibition at the Aca and Heller Galleries, New York, 1958)

**Four figures on the beach, 1957**
Oil on paper mounted on canvas,
94 x 101 cm
Hirshhorn Museum and Sculpture
Garden, Smithsonian Institution,
Washington.
(Gift of Joseph H. Hirshhorn, 1966)

Catalogue raisonné,
vols. II and IV: no. 57/12

"In those sunsets on the lake, and on the farms, on the tiles of the roofs, on the woods, on the chestnut trees, on Varese, on Velate, and all the whole earth, the present author feels bound, imprisoned, and loved as if he were part of it or had been part of it, while these things were taking place and Guttuso, with a supreme slow motion effect, requiring rapidity and rapacity in the eye, when they are meant to become calm, true and great poetry, was reinventing them on the canvas."
(Giovanni Testori, in the catalogue of Guttuso in Varese, Varese, Lativa, 1984)

**Roofs at Velate in winter, 1957**
Oil on canvas, 59 x 72 cm
Signed and dated bottom left
Private Collection

Catalogue raisonné,
vols. II and IV: no. 57/126
Tübingen, 1991

"In his last Rome exhibition Guttuso showed a smoker, a portrait of a man who was a prisoner of his own adversities and uneasiness, bent forwards. In this picture the judgment on the character is determined by very violent notes in both design and colour. Some blacks emphasise the torment of the eyelids and jaw and creep into the bitter yellow pigment in the face. The uneasy characterisation, interrupted by the grey of the jacket, is born again, just as alive or even more so, in the nervous movement of the fingers handling the box of matches and the cigarette."
(Duilio Morosini, *Renato Guttuso*, Cusmano, Rome, 1961)

**The smoker, 1958**
Oil on canvas, 80 x 70 cm
Signed bottom right
On the verso signed and dated
"Guttuso 17 3 58"
Banca di Roma

Catalogue raisonné,
vols. II and IV: no. 58/10

"Always a cigarette between his fingers, one after another consumed nervously in a few puffs; always that veil of smoke in front of his face, as in the self-portraits. Guttuso accompanies the half-sung song, makes it rise up in the gesture of the hand, in the agitated spiral of smoke rising from the cigarette." (Leonardo Sciascia, "Guttuso in Palermo", *Galleria*, XXI, 1-5, Sciascia, Caltanissetta, 1971)

**The smoker, 1958**
Oil on canvas, 98 x 82 cm
Signed bottom centre
Private Collection

Catalogue raisonné,
vols. II and IV: no. 58/17

"Guttuso's indebtedness to the advanced painting of our century is, then, not a concession to modishness, but, on the contrary, a consequence of his overwhelming desire to create a representational art adequate to modern reality. In pursuit of this aim he has, as one might expect, contracted debts in an eclectic and highly personal fashion. Guttuso owes to Picasso and Léger the capacity to simplify form, without losing pictorial depth. (...) Guttuso shows that he has grasped one of the most important and revolutionary lessons of cubist painting: namely, that the realism of a picture can be enhanced by emphasising the reality of painting". (Richard Wollheim, in the catalogue of the exhibition at Roberts & Tunnards Galleries, London 1960)

**Three smokers, 1958**
Oil on canvas, 71 x 85 cm
Signed and dated bottom right
and also top right
Private Collection

Catalogue raisonné,
vol. II: no. 58/13

**Still life with hammer and fork, 1958**
Oil on canvas, 55 x 65 cm
Signed bottom left
On the verso signed and dated
"Guttuso 61"
Private Collection

Catalogue raisonné,
vols. II and IV: no. 58/103

"Guttuso's new painting is direct painting, like flesh laid bare, without any convenient or fallback solutions, without creasing, rubbing, scraping, veiling; painting which looks clean, scrutinised; painting, in short; with a palette of living colours, reds, blues, yellows, whites, which, especially in some wonderful still lifes, are firm, compact, objective, and agive off a dazzling light." (Mario De Micheli, *L'Unità*, 20-2-59)

---

**Trees at Velate, 1958**
Oil on canvas, 75 x 89 cm
Signed bottom right
On the verso "Alberi 1958"
Private Collection

Catalogue raisonné,
vols. II and IV: no. 58/120

"But what appears to me to be new in Guttuso's painting, by comparison with his earlier works, is that the pictorial narration is now entrusted more to objects than to the narrative intention. This is the case in *Trees at Velate* and in other works such as those conducted with intellectual vigour which find immediate expression in the pictorial image." (Marco Valsecchi, *Il Giorno*, 25-2-59)

---

**A wood at Velate, 1958**
Oil on canvas, 119 x 119 cm
Signed and dated in the verso
"Guttuso V. sett ott 58"
Private Collection

Catalogue raisonné,
vol. IV: no. 58/140

"Guttuso paints out of a sense of urgency, because he has something to say, but unlike most of the younger generation his painting is not introvert but extrovert and relates to the world in which we live. What is more, he uses a pictorial language of our own time. It is this which gives his work validity. Guttuso has no claim to being an experimental painter, and we should look not for stylistic innovations in his work. His originality resides above all in his independence, in the freshness and individuality of his vision, in his very personal and expressive use of sharp, bright colours, and above all in his conscientious attempt to evolve a pictorial language which is modern and international (but not a facile Esperanto like the "abstract idiom"), yet at the same time intelligent, and intelligibile.... (Douglas Cooper, in the catalogue of the exhibition at the Aca and Heller Galleries, New York 1958)

---

**Prickly pears, 1959**
Oil on canvas, 100 x 125 cm
Signed and dated bottom right
Galleria d'Arte Moderna e
Contemporanea 'Renato Guttuso'
di Villa Cattolica, Bagheria

Catalogue raisonné,
vols. II and IV: no. 59/126
Tübingen, 1991

"If we look at the series of paintings we will find Sicily present not only as the object represented but as a determining content in planes and various forms.
In them we find the first cultural environment and the first contact with the painting tradition of which there remains the memory and the sign in all his subsequent experience; and the need for a break and a long journey through reality to return thereby making it true. In them we find the figurative and representational capacity of the gesture, the shout, the possibility of synthesis taken outside. Lastly, in them we find total and understanding participation becoming identification with the proletariat and peasant world in Sicily, with its antitheses, its leaps in potential, its compressed strength, the simultaneity of its conditions, its heritage, its future and its historical value. Here we have a portrait of things in Sicily, whose complexity does not need formal decompositions: carters, (...), the sun, the thorns of the prickly pear plant." (Carlo Levi, in catalogue of exibition, *La Sicilia nella pittura di Guttuso*, Bagheria, 1962)

---

**The discussion, 1959-60**
Tempera, oil and collage on canvas,
220 x 250 cm
Signed bottom right "Guttuso"
Tate Gallery. Purchased 1961.

Catalogue raisonné,
vols. II and IV: no. 59-60/1

"*The discussion* is a big canvas over two metres high and two and a half metres wide, which provokes in the spectator a very strong impact with material concreteness: both in the collage diagonal, afterwards spreading out top right and establishing a concrete physical reference to a plane supporting the scene."
(Enrico Crispolti, Catalogue raisonné, vol. II)

"In Guttuso's pictures utensils, tools, instruments, industrial products made in series replace wickerwork baskets, olives and flowers, fruit and other country produce. Guttuso felt urbanisation like an alienating phenomenon, one of extraneousness of the old countryman in a world in which things made in series are worth nothing and do not last: in the morning an intact can made of shining metal, with its fine label well glued on, in the evening a dirty wreck lacerated by the tin-opener, filthy, empty and clinking on a heap of suburban trash." (Alberto Moravia, *Renato Guttuso*, Il Punto, Palermo 1962)
"So it is with those objects in the studio: and there are some done in 61 and 63, they are jars, even Morandi's flasks, but with so much ink, so much black and so many flashes, bitter, acid, boiling tones that scorch like molten sealing wax, or cut you dead like a blade on the forehead. It is there that there is the most authentic Guttuso, on the perilous edge of a form which he wants almost as much as he gloriously pretends to rip it to pieces." (Cesare Brandi, "La mostra di Guttuso a Parma", *Il Punto*, 2, 14, 1964)

**Corner of the studio, 1961**
Oil and tempera on paper on canvas,
180 x 229 cm
Signed and dated bottom right
Private Collection

Catalogue raisonné,
vols. II and IV: no. 61/46

"When he deals with a female nude, for example, with that brutality that Moravia and Pasolini have pointed out, Guttuso - as Modigliani too did in his own way - faces that reality which is most difficult to show because most desirable: that of the body. Undressed or undressing, lying on their backs, with their skirts raised, sleeping, prostrate, consenting, offered, provoking, submissive, Guttuso's women are first of all taken as slaves of male desire: one may wonder whether he totally identifies them with the victims of social injustice and contempt. But at the same time he does not forget the pleasure, the love, the joy that they can arouse, and some of his nudes are among the most voluptuous that I know. One feels an invincible warmth irradiating from them, which causes the barriers of pudency and seemliness to creak." (Alain Jouffroy, "Hope against hope", presentation in the catalogue of the exhibition at the Acquavella Galleries, New York, 1983)

**Nude, 1961**
Oil on canvas, 92 x 73.5 cm
Signed bottom right
On the verso signed and dated
"Guttuso 61"
Private Collection, Alessandria

Catalogue raisonné,
vols. II: no. 61/77
Finale Ligure,1995

"Prickly pears are an aesthetic find by definition, seeing the nearness of the vantage point from which they are observed, which, isolating them from the context of the landscape, almost makes them a mere arabesque, an abstraction of forms....
This shower of prickly pears filling the sheet or the entire picture as if they were infinite are executed with a pulse which is heavy, harsh, inelegant, almost functional, unpleasant, that of a realistic sketch." (Pier Paolo Pasolini, presentation in the catalogue of the exhibition at the Nuova Pesa Gallery, Rome, 1961)

**Prickly pears, 1962**
Oil on canvas, 116 x 90 cm
Signed bottom right "Guttuso"
Private Collection Mario Bocchi, Parma

Catalogue raisonné,
vols. II and IV: no. 62/37
Finale Ligure, 1995

Via Leonina is an old street in Rome, at the centre of the ancient Suburra, which Guttuso saw from his studio, at that time on the top floor of a building in Via Cavour.

"Even with no belief in inspiration one would say that it was painted in a state of grace. The theme takes us back to the first Rome roofs done by Guttuso in 1942: but here the theme is enlarged, developed with quite different authority. Here infact the lesson of Cubism has had its time and weight: and not only the Cubism of Picasso but the Orphic Cubism of Léger. The colour range, through red, pink and orange, is open, intense, luminous. The composition is cunningly composed as regards empty spaces as much as full ones." (Vittorio Rubiu, in *Guttuso*, Sansoni, Florence, 1982, Catalogue of the exhibition at Palazzo Grassi, Venice)

**Roofs in the Via Leonina, 1962**
Oil on canvas, 162 x 130 cm
Signed and dated bottom right
Archivi Guttuso, Rome

Catalogue raisonné,
vols. I and IV: no. 62/113
Tübingen, 1991

"and these prickly pear leaves like prehistoric animals with sucker papillae" (Cesare Brandi, presentation in the catalogue of the exhibition at the Marlborough Fine Art, London, 1979)

**Cactus, 1962**
Oil on canvas, 146 x 114 cm
Private Collection

Catalogue raisonné,
vols. II and IV: no. 62/38

**Still life, 1963**
Oil on canvas, 130 x 130 cm
Signed bottom right
On the verso signed and dated
"Guttuso 63"
Private Collection

Catalogue raisonné,
vols. II and IV: no. 63/48
Tübingen, 1991

"The decomposition and composition of planes according to a pure sculptural criterion of bringing objects all equally into the forefront are the procedures which now come most naturally to him. But already, in these pictures, he introduces light 'fugues', spaces of pure chromatic vibration, which without being naturalistic have a real consistency. In this space objects move forward or backwards in accordance with a different dimension, aided by a simultaneous multiplicity of points of view. In his search for movement and expressive efficacy. Guttuso used foreshortening and irregular planes, but in the past while there they were mainly connected to the expressionist taste, whereas here they help to serve a new lyrical definition of space."
(Mario De Micheli, *Guttuso*, E.I.T., Milan, 1966)

**Cart with cauliflowers, 1973**
Oil on canvas, 142 x 130 cm
Signed bottom right
Private Collection

Catalogue raisonné,
vols. I and IV: no. 73/42
Tübingen, 1991

"The decoration of the cart, the sculptures with which it is adorned, the figurations and pictorial narrations on its sides, respond to a different need than mere embellishment, the will to render 'rich' and precious the most humble practical object (which is characteristic of folk decoration), and affects the realm of fantasy, culture, melodrama, history." (Renato Guttuso, "Sul carretto siciliano." Fiuggi Prize, Fiuggi, 1984)

"I remember carters at night, their songs, about streets and prison.
At times I forgot about school and went with them, all day from dawn till evening,
I learnt more and more to know their problems, their anger, in these excursions
I also did drawings, faces, lemons, asses and mules, hoes, rifles."
(Renato Guttuso, "Una scelta di vita", Fiuggi Prize, op. cit.)

**The Vucciria, 1974**
Oil on canvas, 300 x 300 cm
Signed and dated bottom right
Università degli Studi di Palermo

Catalogue raisonné,
vols. I and IV: no. 74/14
Tübingen, 1991

"The 'Vucciria', as many know, is a Palermo market, nobody knows whether more Arab or Italian, hence very Italian by convention, and also international. Guttuso painted, indeed constructed or reconstructed this market, and gave us his finest Italian painting: showing or demonstrating with the sentiment of art that the international convention coincides with the reality of our country. No other picture by Guttuso - yet his landscapes, his portraits, and his Italian still lifes are so many - ever expressed with so much intensity the profound sentiment of our country."
(Goffredo Parise, Presentation of the exhibition at the Toninelli Gallery, Rome, 1975)

"This is an old idea; I don't even know myself how long I've had it in me. I remember the 'Vucciria' as a boy, when I came from Bagheria to study in Palermo. I went down the steps in Via Roma, entered Piazza Caracciolo and came out in Piazza San Domenico. This breath of folk air, the sounds, the lights, were enough to change the register of my mind. Without knowing, perhaps without even wanting, there were impressed in my retina those cane baskets, in which there were triumphs of fruit, big banquets of fish spread out in a semicircle on the fishmongers' marble counters.
And when I began painting, among the first things there were those colours, those cuts of light, perhaps the same cut as the composition."
(Giuseppe Servello, interview with Renato Guttuso, *Giornale di Sicilia*, 10-12-1974)

**The Breaker's Yard, 1979**
Tempera and acrylic on paper mounted
on canvas, 97 x 139 cm
Signed and dated bottom centre
Private Collection, Florence

Catalogue raisonné,
vols. I and IV: no. 79/24

"A funereal tone, perhaps even intenser, hovers over the carcases of cars, with the empty eye sockets of skulls: and here one can verify - precisely with the yardstick of a natural vision which is certainly not rare - the enhancement and intensification of the spectacle depicted. Not so much because in these car cemeteries it is as if consumer civilisation exposed its wounds, in an allegory of the emptiness of existence, but because in the paintings of cars there is a sense of the indestructibility of evil. Those cars no longer serve any purpose, everything in them has been taken away, no one knows where to put all those carcases: but in Guttuso they become painting as they become sculpture in Chamberlain and César." (Cesare Brandi, presentation in the catalogue of the exhibition at the Marlborough Gallery, London, 1979)

"The theme of the roof, which is so recurrent, does not in the least belong to the pictorial and characteristic repertory of the view. The roof is where you live, the home, hence shelter, and also a prison, if everyone is, even before being the master, a prisoner of his roof and private sphere, molested by his own irrationality. The night does not bring peace there but besieges the collapsing roof, with its monstrous symbols which are the projection of an anguished sleep of ours, of our *dédoublement*, of our daily yielding to the devastating impact of anxiety and desire.
After these allegories, these intense registers of black, it is instructive to revisit Guttuso's painting, and not only that which presents the most immediate link with them, like the battered still life, again on the roof, of the same intense blackness with the exhibited hallmarks of a classic but invented *vanitas*: a very fine thing in which the overturning of depth towards the surface causes the deranged objects to roll down to the tragic and trembling arresting place of the skull." (Maurizio Calvesi, presentation of the catalogue of the exhibition at the Milione Gallery, Milan, 1980)

**Skulls and ties, 1979**
Oil on canvas, 80 x 95 cm
Signed and dated bottom right
Private Collection

Catalogue raisonné,
vols. III and IV: no. 79/24

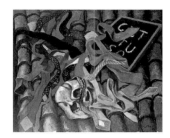

"And painters? Painters dream with the pencil and colours. This is how erotic drawings come into being... Guttuso, instead of dreaming of them, as most people do, throws them down on paper, with the confident stroke that is customary in him, and achieves, in those who look at the compositions, effects and resonances, so that one cannot but recognise his great mastery, even in drawing dreams. Many are lascivious, even coarse women, in whom not only modesty has disappeared, but there is satisfaction at having renounced all modesty. These are the women that frighten the adolescent, or the child about to become an adolescent, but who as a whole exert all the attraction of this abandonment of all pudency.... Often these women have no face. They have no face because they are females and not women,"
(Cesare Musatti, *I disegni erotici di Guttuso*, Mazzotta, Milan, 1980)

**Nude, 1980**
Acrylic and oil on paper mounted on canvas, 99 x 76 cm
Signed bottom right
Private Collection

Catalogue raisonné,
vol. III: no. 80/14

Renato Guttuso never answered the phone himself but, when it rang, waite feverishly for the moment when he would be told who had called and why. During his brief and rare telephone calls, he smoked feverishly, filling any sheet he could get hold of with sketches and little portraits.

**Telephones, 1980**
Oil on canvas, 100 x 90 cm
Galleria d'Arte Nuova Gissi, Turin

Catalogue raisonné,
vols. III and IV: no. 80/33
Turin, 1992

"Guttuso rarely has recourse to the flattery of fascination, rarely chooses the indefinite, the indeterminate, or entrusts meaning to an ineffable emanation.
This time he has done this, listening to the voice of that part of himself which in the most subdued manner murmurs to him 'melancholy was always my companion', and this too is a sign of his courage, his sincerity, his vitality:
of the continual possibility of renewal in his painting."
(Giuliano Briganti, Preface to the exhibition at the Rondanini Gallery, Rome, 1980)

"In a painting what is underneath is always more important. A canvas - a good canvas, I mean - always has a magic mysterious zone, a recondite meaning. Which may be a secret of the painter's or the reflection of a state of mind..."
with Renato Guttuso by Alberigo Segàla, *Epoca*, 4 March 1983)

**Evening at Velate, 1980**
Oil on canvas, cm110 x 90
Signed bottom centre
On the verso signed and dated
Archivi Guttuso, Rome

Catalogue raisonné,
vols. III and IV: no. 80/37
Turin, 1992

"At Velate he has found the opportunity to work more intensely, calmly, continuously. The different environment does not distract him from his themes and characters. Mayakovskii used to say that when he wanted to write verses about silence he took a bus in a central street in Moscow at the rush hour. It seems that for Guttuso too something similar happens, though in an upside-down way: that is to say, in the silence of Velate he has succeeded in painting some of his strongest, most impetuous and dramatic pictures. But at least in the landscapes Velate has produced silence, sweetness, calm and severe, severe and sweet painting."
(Mario De Micheli, *Guttuso*, E.I.T., Milan, 1966)

**Meadow at Velate
with hortensias, 1984**
Oil on canvas, 125 x 147.5 cm
Signed bottom right
Private Collection

Catalogue raisonné,
vol. IV: 84/43

# Biography

*Fabio* **Carapezza Guttuso**

## 1911

Renato Guttuso was born on 26 December 1911 at Bagheria, a small town near Palermo. The Villa Palagonia, the most famous of Bagheria's numerous 18th century villas, appears in his paintings of the sixties. His father Gioacchino, a land-surveyer and amateur watercolourist, and his mother Giuseppina d'Amico, registered the birth on 2 January 1912 (in Sicily, the late registration of males was a means of delaying military service). Guttuso discovered painting early on through his father's watercolours, the studio of the painter Domenico Quattrociocchi and the workshop of the cart painter Emilio Murdolo: "my path was taking shape when I was six, seven, ten years old...".

## 1924–31

In 1924, when Guttuso was thirteen, he began signing

The young Guttuso in Bagheria, early 1930s.

*opposite*
Guttuso in his Piazza Melozzo da Forli studio, c. 1938. Photograph by Eugene Haas.

and dating his work, mainly copies of 19th century Sicilian landscapes. He frequented the studio of the futurist painter Pippo Rizzo (among others) in Palermo and in 1928 took part in a group show there. In 1930 he enrolled in the law faculty at the University of Palermo and also began writing on art. The next year, following the acceptance of two paintings by the Prima Quadriennale d'Arte Nazionale in Rome, he decided to devote himself to painting.

Guttuso with Alberto Moravia, Enzo Siciliano and Dacia Maraini, 1950s.

## 1932–33

In 1932, an exhibition by Guttuso and five other Sicilian artists at the Galleria del Milione, Milan, was reviewed by Carlo Carra and led to the formation of the Group of Four (with sculptors Giovanni Barbera, Nino Franchina and the painter Lia Pasqualino Noto). Their work was a reaction against the dominant 'Novecento' movement. In the course of this year, Guttuso was employed as a picture restorer by the Sovrintendenza dell'Arte Medioevale e Moderna in Umbria. In 1933 he wrote his first article on Picasso and one on Scipione. While in Rome Guttuso met Corrado Cagli, Mario Mafai, Mirko Basaldella and Percile Fazzini. To earn his living, he worked as a window dresser for the department store Rinascente.

## 1934–36

In 1935, Guttuso did his military service in Milan where he made friends with artists associated with the group 'Corrente' (including Lucio Fontana with whom he shared a studio) and the poet Salvatore Quasimodo and the philosopher Antonio Banfi. The Milan period was marked by depression and severe economic hardship (reflected in the tone of his poetry of the period).

Guttuso with Elio Vittorini in the Velate studio, Varese, in front of The discussion, 1960.

## 1937–39

After settling permanently in Rome in 1937, Guttuso's studio, first in Piazza Melozzo da Forlì and from 1940 in the via Pompeo Magno, became the centre for artists and writers, including Alberto Moravia, Antonello Trombadori and Libero De Libero.

His friendships with Trombadori and Mario Alicata played a decisive role in his decision to join the Communist Party. His writing and painting became increasingly committed to a realism based on contemporary events. A series of large works, *Fucilazione in campagna* (*Execution in the country*) dedicated to Garcia Lorca, and *Fuga dall'Etna* (*Flight from Etna*) which won the Bergamo award in 1940, established the artist's international reputation. 'Il Selvaggio' devoted an issue to his drawings (November 1939). In 1938 he met Mimise Dotti who became his life-long companion.

## 1940–44

The group of young Roman intellectuals with whom Guttuso was associated took an anti-fascist position and aligned themselves with the Italian Communist Party. He painted landscapes (many with Sicilian themes), nudes and still lifes as well as large-scale compositions like *Crocifissione* (*Crucifixion*) (finished in 1941 and shown in the officially endorsed Premio Bergamo in the Autumn of 1942). This painting provoked widespread controversy to the extent that the Vatican threatened to excommunicate visitors to the exhibition. Nevertheless, despite the furore and his criticism of the regime Guttuso was accorded official recognition. In 1943, forced to leave Rome for political reasons, he took refuge with Alberto

Guttuso with Max Ernst in the S. Chiara Cloister, Naples, 1965.

Guttuso with Picasso at Mougins in 1965.

Della Ragione at Quarto, near Genoa, before returning to join the Resistance. Works like *Trionfo della morte* (*The Triumph of Death*) reflect his experience of the partisans' struggles against the Germans. The drawings *Gott Mit Uns*, shown in an exhibition sponsored by *l'Unità* and later reproduced clandestinely in an album in early 1945, also bear witness to this period.

Guttuso during the making of the Newsstand, 1965.

### 1945–50

In 1946 Guttuso moved to a new studio in the Via Margutta, Rome. The same year he met Picasso in Paris and their friendship lasted until Picasso's death. With Renato Birolli, Emilio Vedova and Giuseppe Marchiori, Guttuso founded the "Fronte Nuovo delle Arti' (New Arts Front), a group of politically aware artists whose work dealt with socially committed subject matter in a post-Cubist style. He was one of the signatories to the 'Manifesto del neo-cubismo' published in the catalogue of their group show at the Galleria del Secolo, Rome, in December 1946 (the manifesto also appeared in *La Fiera Litteraria*, 9 January 1947). In 1947 he began working in the Villa Massimo, where many other painters also had their studios.

Guttuso with Eduardo De Filippo, 1960s.

Guttuso contributed regularly to *l'Unità*, *Vie Nuove* and *Rinascita*. In 1948 he was made a member of the World Council of Peace at the Congress of Peace held in Warsaw. An important group of works were shown in the XXIX Venice Biennale in 1948 (and reviewed by critics like Douglas Cooper who helped introduce his work in London in an exhibition at the Hanover Gallery). At the 1950 Venice Biennale Guttuso showed *Occupazione delle terre incolte in Sicilia*, one of his most ambitious paintings to date.

## 1951–56

Guttuso was involved in numerous projects for the theatre as well the major exhibition of Picasso in Rome in 1953. His work was shown in the Venice Biennale in 1952, 1954 and 1956. In 1952, the Patriarch of Venice brought pressure on the President of the XXVI Venice Biennale to prevent the inclusion of *Crucifixion* 1940-41 in the one-man show of Guttuso's work in the Italian pavilion. His work was promoted by John Berger and Peter de Francia at the time of his 1955 exhibition at the Leicester Galleries, London.

Guttuso with Anna Magnani.

## 1957–65

Guttuso was especially active as an art critic, contributing articles on the theory of art and on major figures (including Permeke and Pollock) for important Italian and international newspapers and magazines such as *Realismo* and *Il Contemporaneo*. He continued his involvement in the theatre, initiating a ten-year collaboration with Aurele Millos. He also made illustrations for *The Divine Comedy* (published by Alberto Mondadori in 1963).

Major exhibitions included those at the Aca-Heller Gallery, New York (introduced by Douglas Cooper, Roberto Longhi and James Thrall Soby) in 1958; at the Pushkin Museum, Moscow and the Hermitage Museum, Leningrad, marked by a debate on Soviet social realism at the Art Academy, in 1961; and a large retrospective at the Stedelijk Museum, Amsterdam, in 1962. That year, drawings for Verdi's *La Forza del Destino* were shown at the McRoberts & Tunnard Gallery, London. In 1963, an exhibition with two hundred works was held at the

Guttuso painting The Funeral of Togliatti, 1972.

Palazzo della Pilotta, Parma (with texts in the catalogue by Longhi, Franco Russoli and Giovanni Testori). Several monographs were published (whose authors included Elio Vittorini, Duilio Morosini and John Berger). Guttuso began working on the theme of the newsstand which led to his only major sculpture, *Edicola*.

Guttuso with Fabio Carapezza and Fabrizio Clerici in Sicily, 1970s.

### 1965–71

In 1965 Guttuso moved to the Palazzo del Grillo, Rome, where he lived and worked until his death. Summers were spent at a villa in Velate, near Varese. He painted the large *Documentario sul Vietnam*, now in Berlin. The following year he realised *Autobiografia*, a large cycle of paintings which constituted the nucleus of an important exhibition which travelled to Berlin, Darmstadt, Recklinghausen, Antwerp, Prague and Hamburg (organised by Bernd Krimmel, Hans Sperlich and Thomas Grokawick) and accompanied by a text by Werner Haftmann. Guttuso worked on scenery for *Il contratto* by his friend Eduardo De Filippo as well as costumes and scenery for *Carmen* (Rome, 1970) and works by Luigi Nono. Werner Spies contributed a text for an exhibition at the Michael Hertz Gallery in Bremen in 1969, in which Guttuso showed the large painting *Figlie di Lot* (*Lot's Daughters*). Carlo Levi introduced a volume on recent drawing and Enrico Crispolti published a monograph on the *Crucifixion*.

Guttuso with Giorgio de Chirico at the Galleria Toninelli, Rome, 1976.

A major retrospective took place at the Palazzo dei Normanni, Palermo, 1971, with catalogue introductions by Leonardo Sciascia and Franco Grasso, and at the Musée d'Art Moderne de la Ville de Paris, 1971 with texts by Antonio Del Guercio and Jacques Lassaigne.

## 1972–80

Guttuso was awarded the Lenin Prize for Peace and Friendship among Peoples at the time of his exhibition at the Art Academy in Moscow, 1972. The same year a large retrospective toured Eastern Europe and an important cycle of commemorative paintings, *Omaggio a Picasso* (*Homage to Picasso*) was shown first in Milan and then in Bremen. *La Vucciria* was completed in 1974, and *Caffè Greco* in 1976; the latter (now in the Ludwig Collection, Cologne) was exhibited at the Michael Hertz Gallery in Bremen in 1977 accompanied by a catalogue introduction by Maurizio Calvesi. Lothar Lang wrote a monograph and Guttuso illustrated Verga's *Malavoglia*, 1978 and Virgil's *Aeneid*, 1980. He showed at Marlborough Fine Art, London, in 1979.

In 1976 he was elected a Senator of the Republic (Senatore della Repubblica nel Collegio di Sciacca).

## 1981–87

In 1981 Guttuso completed another important cycle of paintings, *Le Allegorie* (*The Allegories*) which was shown first in Rome (with an introduction by Giuliano Briganti) and then at the Galleria d'Arte Moderna, Bologna. He also painted nudes, themes of daily life and works in homage to Courbet, Dürer, Raphael, as well as variations on paintings by Antonello da Messina and Dosso Dossi. In 1982, the Palazzo Grassi, Venice, organised an important exhibition and the following year Guttuso showed recent work at the Acquavella Galleries, New York (including the large canvas *Spes contra Spem* (*Hope against Hope*, which was the subject of an article by Giovanni Testori). In 1983, he painted a mural, *Fuga in*

Guttuso with Federico Fellini in Rome, 1979.

Maurizio Calvesi, Marcello Carapezza and Renato Guttuso, 1985.

*Egitto* (*The Flight into Egypt*), for one of the chapels of Sacro Monte (above Varese, near Guttuso's villa at Velate). The same year, he completed a cycle of paintings on the theme of female gymnasts and football players which was shown in 1984 in an exhibition organised by the Olympic Committee in Rome and then Los Angeles. In 1985, with the assistance of Amadeo Brogli, he painted a 129 sq. metre ceiling made up of fourteen panels reprasenting the legend of Cola Pesce for the Teatro Vittorio Emanuele in Messina.

Guttuso in his Palazzo del Grillo studio in Rome, 1970s.

At the end of 1984, the first three volumes of the catalogue raisonné compiled by Enrico Crispolti were published by Giorgio Mondadori Associati, Milan (the fourth was issued in 1990). These are the major source of biographical and bibliographical information.

Guttuso died on 18 January 1987 at his home in the Palazzo del Grillo, leaving major works to the Galleria d'Arte Moderna, Rome and a collection of graphics and paintings to his native town of Bagheria which are now housed in the Villa Cattolica as part of the Museo Guttuso. A large funerary monument by Giacomo Manzù, a close friend of the artist's, stands in the grounds. In 1987 memorial exhibitions were held in Bagheria and Verona.

Under the direction of his adopted son, Fabio Carapezza Guttuso, an archive was established in the artist's former studio in the Palazzo del Grillo. Dr.Carapezza Guttuso has since collaborated on numerous exhibitions, including a presentation in Germany which toured in 1991-92 and one devoted to his theatrical sketches shown at La Scala.

# Exhibitions and Bibliography

Archivi Guttuso

## A - PRINCIPAL EXHIBITIONS

*Renato Guttuso*, Galleria Genova, Genoa, January 1940. Catalogue: text by A. Moravia.

*Renato Guttuso*, Galleria dello Zodiaco, Rome, January 1943. Catalogue: text by G. Severini.

*Renato Guttuso, «Gott mit uns»*, Galleria La Margherita, Rome, 1945. Catalogue: text by A. Trombadori.

*Renato Guttuso*, Galleria La Margherita, Rome, 1946. Catalogue: text by L. Venturi.

*Renato Guttuso – Catherine Yarrow*, The Hanover Gallery, London, 1 June-1 July 1950. Catalogue: text by D. Cooper.

*Guttuso*, Galleria La Colonna, Milan, 4-17 December 1952. Catalogue: text by R. De Grada.

*Renato Guttuso*, Bucharest 1954.

*Renato Guttuso kiàllitasa*, Budapest 1954.

*Renato Guttuso*, Vystavni Sine Manesa, Prague, 15 January -14 February 1954. Catalogue: texts by P. Neruda and A. Trombadori.

*Renato Guttuso*, Centralne Bjuro Wystaw Artysty Cznych, Warsaw, February 1954.

*Guttuso*, Leicester Galleries, March 1955. Catalogue: text by J. Berger.

*Guttuso*, Aca and Heller Galleries, New York, 7-28 April 1958. Catalogue: texts by D. Cooper and R. Longhi.

*Renato Guttuso*, Galleria del Milione, Milan, 19 February-7 March 1959. Catalogue: text by F. Russoli.

*Guttuso*, McRoberts & Tunnard Ltd, London, 1960. Catalogue: text by R. Wollheim.

*Guttuso*, Hermitage, Leningrad, 1961; Pushkin Museum, Moscow, 1961; Novosibirsk, 1961. Catalogue: texts by A. Trombadori and M. Alicata.

*Guttuso*, Stedelijk Museum, Amsterdam, 9 November-10 December 1962; Palais des Beaux-Arts, Charleroi, 12 January-3 February 1963.

*La Sicilia nella pittura di Renato Guttuso*, Comune di Bagheria, 21 October-5 November 1962. Catalogue: texts by C. Levi and M. Penelope.

*Nuove opere di Renato Guttuso*, Galleria La Nuova Pesa, Rome, 1962. Catalogue: text by A. Trombadori.

*Renato Guttuso: Mostra antologica dal 1931 ad oggi*, Palazzo della Pilotta, Parma, 15 December 1963-31 January 1964. Catalogue: texts by R. Longhi, F. Russoli and G. Testori.

*Renato Guttuso: Opere, acquarelli, disegni dal 1940 al 1966*. Nationalgalerie Berlin, 18 February-2 April 1967; Museum der bildenden Künste, Leipzig, May 1967. Catalogue: texts by C. Levi and P.H. Feist.

*Renato Guttuso*, Kunstverein Darmstadt, 26 August-4 October 1967; Städtische Kunsthalle Recklinghausen, 22 October-26 November 1967. Catalogue: text by B. Krimmel.

*Guttuso*, Hochschule für bildende Künste, Hamburg, 22 April-31 May 1968; Koninlijk Museum voor Schone Kunste, Antwerp, January 1968. Catalogue: text by B. Krimmel.

*Renato Guttuso: Immagini autobiografiche ed altre opere*, Palazzo dei Diamanti, Ferrara, 11 July-8 September 1968.

*Renato Guttuso: Autobiograficky Cyklus*, Národní Galerie v Praze, Waldstejnská Jizdarná, Prague 1968. Catalogue: text by J. Kotalik.

*Mostra Antologica dell'opera di Renato Guttuso*, Palazzo dei Normanni, Palermo, 13 February-14 March 1971. Catalogue: texts by L. Sciascia, F. Russoli and F. Grasso.

*Renato Guttuso*, Musée d'Art Moderne de la Ville de Paris, 30 September-1 November 1971. Catalogue: texts by J. Lassaigne and A. Del Guercio.

*Guttuso*, Neue Gesellschaft für bildende Kunst, Berlin, February-March 1972. Catalogue: poems by Pier Paolo Pasolini, Rafael Alberti, Pablo Neruda; texts by G. Bock, G. Caronello, M. Grassi, A.D. Gorella, P. Hielscher and K. Sello.

*Renato Guttuso*, Hermitage, Leningrad, 1972; Musej Akademij Chudozestv SSSR, Moscow, 1972. Catalogue: text by V. Gorjainov.

*Guttuso. Das Gastmahl*, Galerie Michael Hertz, Bremen, November-December 1973. Catalogue: text by W. Schmied.

*Renato Guttuso: Obrazy z let 1931-1971*, Národní Galerie v Praze, Prague, January-February 1973.

*Renato Guttuso*, Muzeul de arta al Republicii Socialiste Romania, Bucharest, May-June 1973. Catalogue: text by M. Deac.

*Renato Guttuso*, Kunsthalle Budapest, 20 March-15 April 1973. Catalogue: text by A. Nora.

*Renato Guttuso*, Galerie Jan Krugier, Geneva, July 1974. Catalogue: text by M. Pianzola.

*Guttuso*, Toninelli Arte Moderna, Rome, March-April 1974. Catalogue: text by W. Schmied.

*Renato Guttuso: Grandi formati*, Il Collezionista d'Arte Contemporanea, Rome, 1975. Catalogue: texts by R. Alberti and P. Neruda.

*Guttuso*, Städtische Kunstgalerie, Sofia, 1976. Catalogue: text by A. Neikov.

*Opere scelte di Renato Guttuso*, Todi, 16 May-13 June 1976. Catalogue: text by A. Trombadori.

*Renato Guttuso, A festö mühelye*, Kossuth Könyvkiadò, Budapest 1977.

*Renato Guttuso: Gemälde und Handzeichnungen*, Kunsthalle Köln, 4 June-24 July 1977. Catalogue: text by S. Gohr.

*Renato Guttuso*, Galleria dello Scudo, Verona, 16 November 1977- January 1978.

*Renato Guttuso*, Moderna Museet, Stockholm, 15 April-28 May 1978. Catalogue: texts by K. Lindegren and A. Ehnmark.

*Renato Guttuso: Recent Paintings, Watercolours and Drawings*, Marlborough Fine Art Ltd., London, 1-24 March 1979. Catalogue: texts by M. Quantrill and C. Brandi.

*Renato Guttuso: Le Allegorie e altre opere recenti*, Galleria Rondanini, Rome, February-March 1981. Catalogue: text by G. Briganti.

*Guttuso: Opere dal 1931 al 1981*, Centro di Cultura di Palazzo Grassi, Venezia, 4 April-20 June 1982. Catalogue: Sansoni Editore, Firenze 1982; texts by C. Brandi, M. Calvesi, V. Rubiu, A. Codognato.

*Guttuso nel disegno: Anni venti/ottanta*, Reggio Emilia, 1983. Catalogue edited by E. Crispolti, Oberon, Rome.

*Renato Guttuso: Recent Paintings, Watercolors and Drawings*, Acquavella Galleries, Inc., New York, 14 April-14 May 1983. Catalogue: texts by J. Richardson and A. Jouffroy.

*Renato Guttuso. Spes contra spem*, Castel Sant'Angelo, Rome, 16 February-16 March 1983. Catalogue edited by C. Benincasa, Mazzotta, Milan 1983; texts by S. Jusco, C. Benincasa and A. Jouffroy.

*Guttuso a Varese*, Musei Civici, Villa Mirabello, Varese, 23 June-30 September 1984. Catalogue: Edizioni Lativa, Varese; texts by G. Testori and S. Colombo.

*Guttuso Grandi opere*, Palazzo Reale, Milan, December 1984-February 1985. Catalogue edited by V. Rubiu, Mazzotta, Milan.

*Renato Guttuso.Il Bosco d'Amore*, Cripta del Collegio dei Gesuiti, Siracusa, 30 March-21 April 1985. Catalogue edited by Fabio Carapezza, Mazzotta, Milan 1985.

*Guttuso a Genova nel nome Della Ragione*, Villa Croce, Genova, October-November 1985. Catalogue edited by L. Caprile, Electa, Milan.

*Guttuso e la Sicilia. Opere dal 1970 ad oggi*, Palazzo Comitini, Palermo, April-May 1985. Catalogue edited by M. Calvesi.

*Guttuso opere dal 1938 al 1985*, Cittadella dei musei, Cagliari 1986. Catalogue: Mazzotta, Milan 1986; texts by V. Rubiu and C. Brandi.

*Guttuso 50 anni di pittura*, Palazzo Forti, Verona, 29 July-15 October 1987. Catalogue edited by G. Cortenova and E. Mascelloni, Mazzotta, Milan 1987.

*Guttuso, dalla Sicilia a Velate*, Villa Tosi, Busto Arsizio, Varese, December 1987-February 1988. Catalogue edited by C. Occhipinti.

*Renato Guttuso dagli esordi al Gott Mit Uns, 1924-1944*, Museo di Villa Cattolica, Bagheria, July 1987; Palazzo Isimbardi, Milan, 29 October-10 January 1988. Catalogue edited by M. Calvesi and D. Favatella Lo Cascio, Sellerio, Palermo; the Catalogue includes an anthology of Guttuso's writings edited by Marco Carapezza.

*Guttuso*, Kunsthalle Tübingen, Kunstmuseum Düsseldorf, Kunstverein Hamburg, 1991-92. Catalogue edited by F. Carapezza Guttuso, Verlag Gerd Hatje, Stuttgart, 1991; texts by M. Calvesi, W. Haftmann, E. Steingräber, S. von Wiese.

*Renato Guttuso al Teatro alla Scala*, Ridotto del Teatro alla Scala, Milan, 1992. Catalogue edited by E. Steingräber, Amici della Scala, Milano; texts by C. Fontana, P. Petraroia, A. Crespi Morbio, M.G. Vaccari, V. Crespi and F. Carapezza Guttuso.

*Guttuso*, Galleria d'Arte Nuova Gissi, Torino, November 1992-January 1993. Catalogue: text by Marco Rosci.

*Renato Guttuso*, , Finale Ligure (La Spezia), 20 October 1995-7 January 1996. Catalogue edited by Luciano Caprile.


## B - BIBLIOGRAPHY

A comprehensive bibliography may be found in *Catalogo Ragionato generale dei dipinti di Renato Guttuso*, edited by Enrico Crispolti, vols. I-IV, Giorgio Mondadori, Milan, 1983-1990.

Giuseppe Marchiori, *Guttuso*, Edizioni Moneta, Milan 1952.

John Berger, *Guttuso*, Veb Verlag der Kunst, Dresden 1957.

Duilio Morosini, *Renato Guttuso*, Cusmano Editore, Rome 1960.

Elio Vittorini, *Guttuso*, Edizioni del Milione, Milan 1960.

John Berger, *Guttuso*, Iskusstvo, Mosca 1962.

Alberto Moravia, Franco Grasso, *Guttuso*, Ed. Il Punto, Palermo 1962.

Mario De Micheli, *Il disegno moderno. Guttuso*, SEDA, Milan 1963.

A.G. Barskaja, J.A. Rusakov, *Renato Guttuso*, Sovetskj Chudoznik, Leningrado-Mosca 1965.

Carlo Levi, *Renato Guttuso trent'anni 1939-1969*, Terenzi, Rome 1969.

Enrico Crispolti, *Guttuso: Crocifissione*, Accademia Editrice, Rome 1970.

Mario De Micheli, *Guttuso. L'occupazione delle terre*, Schubert Editore, Milan 1970.

Renato Guttuso, *Mestiere di pittore. Scritti sull'arte e la società*, De Donato, Bari 1972.

Werner Haftmann, *Guttuso: Autobiographische Bilder*, Propyläen, Frankfurt a.M.-Berlin-Wien 1971.

Natale Tedesco, edited by, *Guttuso*, monographic issue of *Galleria*, XXI, 1-5, 1971.

Mario De Micheli, edited by, *Renato Guttuso: la vita e le opere*, Edizioni Capitol, Bologna 1974.

Lothar Lang, *Renato Guttuso*, Welt der Kunst, Henschelverlag Kunst und Gesellschaft, Berlino 1975.

Mario De Micheli, *Guttuso*, Vanessa, Milan 1976.

Giorgio Soavi, *Nei luoghi di Guttuso. Viaggio in Sicilia, Roma e Velate*, Franca May Edizioni, Rome 1979.

*Omaggio a Renato Guttuso*, Parigi 1981. Texts by B. Joppolo, R. Alberti, C. Brandi, G. Briganti, M. Calvesi, A. Del Guercio, W. Haftmann, R. Longhi, A. Moravia, P. Neruda, P.P. Pasolini, J. Rewald, F. Russoli, L. Sciascia, R. Tassi, G. Ungaretti, D. Cooper.

Franco Grasso, *Renato Guttuso: pittore di Bagheria*, Tringale Editore, Catania 1982.

Cesare Brandi, *Guttuso*, Gruppo Editoriale Fabbri, Milan 1983.

Enrico Crispolti, *Leggere Guttuso*, A. Mondadori editore, Milan 1987.

*Manzù a Guttuso*, edited by F. Carapezza Guttuso, Novecento, Palermo 1990.

Maurizio Calvesi, Dora Favatella Lo Cascio *Museo Guttuso. Catalogo del museo Guttuso di Bagheria*, Novecento, Palermo 1991.

Vincenzo Consolo, L'enorme realtà, Arte e Dossier, no. 63, December 1991, Giunti, Firenze.

Printed in april 1996
by Priulla s.r.l. - Palermo